THE Aftermath OF THE Anglo-Zulu War

MATTHEW S. WELTIG

Twenty-First Century Books   MINNEAPOLIS

Consultant: Trevor Getz, associate professor of history at San Francisco State University and a 2008
Fulbright scholar at the University of Western Cape and University of Stellenbosch in South Africa

*The image on the jacket and the cover is of a group of Zulu warriors wearing traditional dress and carrying
shields. The photo dates to 1888. (Photo © Bettmann/CORBIS)*

Twenty-First Century Books
A division of Lerner Publishing Group, Inc.
241 First Avenue North
Minneapolis, MN 55401 U.S.A.

Website address: www.lernerbooks.com

Library of Congress Cataloging-in-Publication Data

Weltig, Matthew Scott.
        The aftermath of the Anglo-Zulu war / by Matthew S. Weltig.
            p.   cm. — (Aftermath of History)
        Includes bibliographical references and index.
        ISBN 978-0-8225-7599-3 (lib. bdg. : alk. paper)
        1. Zulu War, 1879—Influence. I. Title.
    DT1875.W45 2009
    968.4′045—dc22   2007050826

Manufactured in the United States of America
1 2 3 4 5 6 – BP – 14 13 12 11 10 09

Contents

Death on the Plains

ZULU PRINCE ZIWEDU and Dutch trader Cornelius Vijn, messengers to the Zulu king Cetshwayo, watched a bloody battle on the morning of July 4, 1879. From their vantage point on a nearby hill, they watched the battle between British and Zulu armies unfold. As the noontime sun shone down on the rolling plains near Ulundi, Cetshwayo's capital (in what is now modern Ulundi in KwaZulu-Natal, South Africa), a terrifying scene confronted them.

Columns of smoke billowed over flames engulfing the Zulu villages and barracks. The capital, with its beehive-shaped wicker huts and its magnificent enclosures for the royal cattle herds, burned and smoldered. Flames also roared within the European-style building that Cetshwayo had built there. The fire consumed its roof and everything inside. As the smoke rolled across the plains, observers could smell the burning wood and grass and the scent of exploding gunpowder in the air.

Around a large, empty patch of trampled grass on the plains, corpses lay strewn amidst discarded cowhide shields, fallen rifles, and abandoned spears. Blood that had flowed from bullet and shrapnel wounds was beginning to dry, forming black patches on bare skin. The Zulu warriors had not worn their battle finery to this confrontation. To ensure freedom of movement, they wore only loincloths, ammunition pouches, and powder horns. The heads of the older men still bore the headrings that were woven into their hair. Here or there a body still bore a necklace or armband that had not been taken as a souvenir. In places where fighting had been most intense, the bodies of Zulu warriors lay piled atop the bodies of their dead comrades. Most of these men had been killed by the fire of British rifles. Farther out, hidden from view by grass and shrubs, lay the bodies of men who had been killed by British rockets and artillery shells.

A large group of British soldiers in bright red coats were calmly resting and eating a meal. They sat on the banks of the Mbilane River

A HAND-COLORED LANTERN SLIDE FROM THE NINETEENTH CENTURY DEPICTS THE JULY 4, 1879, BATTLE OF ULUNDI BETWEEN ZULU AND BRITISH FORCES IN ZULULAND.

within sight of the battlefield. Most felt certain that their fighting for the day was done. Those few who had been wounded by Zulu rifle shots were being cared for by medics. In the empty center of the battlefield, a dozen patches of bare earth covered the graves of the few British soldiers to have died in the battle.

The killing had not ended, but smaller groups of British soldiers on horseback would complete the job while their fellows rested. The mounted soldiers searched the tall grass of the plains, the ravines, and the riverbanks for hidden Zulu warriors. They stabbed those they found with lances, slashed them with swords, or shot them with pistols. Other British horsemen pursued fleeing Zulu warriors into the hills. Known for their bravery and extreme fierceness, the Zulu warriors generally fought to the death. When they ran out of bullets, they turned to their spears, clubs, and shields. Only two Zulu warriors were captured by the British troops that day. Those who did not flee, or who did not flee fast enough, were killed. This brutal and bloody battle marked the end of the Anglo-Zulu War and decisively confirmed British dominance in the Zulu kingdom.

CHAPTER 1

The Anglo-Zulu War

THE ANGLO-ZULU WAR of 1879 was the last war fought by the independent Zulu nation against an external enemy. But it was far from the first. The Zulu people—a group that had lived in southeastern Africa since its establishment in the sixteenth century—grew to be a powerful kingdom in southeastern Africa through a series of wars of expansion fought under its first king, Shaka (ca. 1787–1828). Shaka's successor, Dingane (ca. 1798–1840), continued to fight against European colonists and other external enemies. His successors, Mpande and Cetshwayo, came to power through civil wars.

In 1816, the Zulu people made up a small group that lived as farmers and cattle-herders to the north of the Tugela River in southeastern Africa. Shaka, one of the chief's sons, had his own half brother killed that same year. He did this to ensure that he would become the next Zulu chief. He seized control of the Zulu group and led

SHAKA, THE FIRST ZULU KING, FORGED THE ZULU NATION THROUGH
WARS OF EXPANSION. THIS IS A NINETEENTH-CENTURY ENGRAVING BY
NATHANIEL ISSACS.

them to conquer or disperse other groups and kingdoms throughout
the region. When Shaka died in 1828, the Zulu kingdom covered
a wide area. It extended north as far as the Pongolo River in what
is now modern South Africa, south to the area around what is now

Durban, South Africa, and from the region's Drakensberg Mountains east to the Indian Ocean.

Shaka's reign ended the same way it began. His half brothers Dingane and Mhlangana stabbed him to death, and Dingane seized power. Dingane feared that he too would be dethroned and assassinated by a relative. So he "commenced his career as king by killing all his brothers, except Panda [Mpande], also his brothers' principal chiefs and friends, with all their women and children; he looked upon his brother Panda as harmless, and so spared him. At least eighty men thus perished," the later Zulu king Cetshwayo recalled.

Dingane made many enemies. They included local African groups such as the powerful Swazi to the north of the Zulu lands. They also included white colonists who were advancing from two directions. From the west came a group of descendants of earlier Dutch colonists who had founded Cape Colony in southwestern Africa in the seventeenth century. The colony was later seized by Great Britain, and many Dutch-speaking colonists had fled, hoping to establish farms independent of British authority. These people came to be called Boers, after the Dutch word for "farmer." To the south of Zululand, as the area that remained in control of the Zulu king came to be called, lay Natal. Port Natal, located where the modern city of Durban stands, began as a small settlement founded by British traders in an area controlled by Shaka. Shaka did not give the land to Britain. Instead, he allowed these traders to live and govern there, much as he allowed other allies and lower Zulu chiefs to do throughout his kingdom. As time went by, more and more Boers settled near the Port Natal settlement, which they eventually would control. As Boers settled in the area, it continued to expand to become a large colony called Natal. Relations between some of these Boers and Dingane grew tense, and as they worsened, Zululand was drawn into armed conflict with both British and Boer settlers.

Rise of the Zulu Nation

IN 1816, Shaka, a son of a Zulu chief, was serving in the army of Dingiswayo, king of the powerful Mthethwa confederation that held sway over the lands north of the Tugela River in southeastern Africa. At that time, the small Zulu group was allied with Dingiswayo's Mthethwa confederation. A talented tactician and military leader, Shaka rose quickly through the ranks of Dingiswayo's army. He became one of Dingiswayo's favorites. Dingiswayo, who had assassinated his younger brother to attain his position, supported Shaka when he had his half-brother Sigujana killed and declared himself the Zulu leader.

At this time, a war raged between the Mthethwa and another powerful chiefdom in the region, the Ndwandwe. The year after Shaka seized the Zulu chieftainship, the Ndwandwe mounted a massive campaign against the Mthethwa. Rather than helping the Mthethwa cause, Shaka held back. Instead, he trained the Zulu warriors in new weapons and tactics that he had been developing under Dingiswayo. Without Zulu assistance, the Mthethwa toppled under the Ndwandwe onslaught.

Shaka, a charismatic and ruthless leader, inspired the Zulu warriors to become the most ferocious fighters in the region. When the Ndwandwe followed up the Mthethwa campaigns with raids on the Zulu, they discovered that they faced fresh, disciplined men. The Zulu warriors had learned from Shaka how to fight more effectively in hand-to-hand combat rather than relying on long-range spear-throwing.

In 1818, the second year of Shaka's reign, the warriors of his small Zulu group defeated a much larger Ndwandwe force that had been sent against them. They then took the offensive, destroying the Ndwandwe capital.

The Zulu military had conquered a major power. The Zulu people in turn became a major power in southeastern Africa. Shaka continued his military expansion until his death in 1828.

However, Dingane's focus on external enemies did not mean that his Zulu rivals were safe. For example, his brother Mpande feared that Dingane might execute him. As a result, Mpande fled to Natal in 1839 along with his son Cetshwayo and his followers.

There, "Panda [Mpande] seems to have made great friends with the Boers," Cetshwayo reported, "and they treated him kindly." Boer groups had fought a number of bloody battles against Dingane's warriors, and they would be glad to see him removed. So in January 1840, Mpande's army, backed by a Boer force, invaded Zululand. Mpande's army led the invasion. The Boers followed behind, keeping Mpande safe from the action but also keeping him under their control. Joined by deserters from Dingane's army, Mpande's forces defeated Dingane without the actual assistance of the Boers. Dingane himself fled and was later killed in the Swazi kingdom.

Although these Boers had not taken part in the battle, they demanded concessions from Mpande before they would recognize him as the Zulu leader and before they would allow him to leave the Boer camp. One of these concessions involved Natal. The Boers required him to give all of Natal to them, which he did, fixing the border of Zululand at the Tugela River and the Drakensberg Mountains. The Zululand established by the Boer group and Mpande was half the size of the lands conquered by Shaka and ruled by Dingane.

Shaka's Revolution

UNDER SHAKA the Zulu people had become a military force recognized throughout southeastern Africa. As boys reached a certain age, they were gathered together into a *butho*, or regiment, with whom they would train and fight. During times of peace, buthos would be called up to do work, such as building royal kraals for the king. Girls were also formed into buthos to do the farming required by the growing kingdom. Shaka prohibited marriage of any of the members of the buthos, male or female, until he granted permission. Men could not marry until Shaka had granted their whole butho the right to wear a headring, the symbol of adulthood. He generally did not grant this right until the men were seasoned warriors, over the age of thirty.

In the end, Mpande's decision to seek Boer help against his brother had long-term consequences. It set in motion events that would draw Zululand into territorial agreements with the colonial powers in Africa that would ultimately swallow up Zululand.

INTERACTIONS WITH THE COLONIES

In 1842 the British conquered Natal. Many of the Boers living in Natal trekked back across the Drakensbergs to escape British rule. They eventually established two independent republics in southern Africa—the South African Republic (Transvaal) and the Orange Free State. Other Boers asked Mpande to allow them to settle on the Zulu side of the Vaal River and in the Utrecht district in northwestern Zululand. Mpande agreed. However, according to Cetshwayo, he "was very glad to see the

The Great Trek

DESCENDANTS OF DUTCH SETTLERS in Cape Colony of southwestern Africa had long resented their British rulers. This resentment sprang from many complex causes. These included British limitations on the independence of people living in Cape Colony and government distribution of farms in part of the colony. In 1834, two occurrences increased this resentment dramatically. First, many Dutch-speaking farmers lost their property as the British waged war against the Xhosa people on a border of the colony. Second, the British abolished slavery in the colony. So for several years following 1834, thousands of Dutch-speakers departed to find farms farther to the north and to the northeast. This movement came to be known as the Great Trek.

Trekkers who established themselves beyond the Orange River in what is now the Free State Province of South Africa established the Orange Free State. Other trekkers continued beyond the Vaal River and founded the South African Republic in the Transvaal.

English take Natal from the Boers; he did not trust the latter, and was always in fear that they would turn on him and make further demands."

The Boers in Zululand soon became unhappy with the arrangement. They wanted more land and continued to establish farms east of the Blood River, the border of Utrecht. They tried to buy the entire area from Mpande, offering him two hundred cattle, but he refused to sell. He did accept one hundred of the cattle, however, as a type of rent for use of the land. This eventually led to a dispute when some Boers claimed that they had bought and therefore owned the land. Zulu leaders claimed that the king had simply allowed the Boers to use it. As a result, armed skirmishes between individual Boers and Zulu fighters occurred in the area throughout Mpande's reign (1840–1872).

STRUGGLE OVER SUCCESSION

Mpande remained king until his death (from natural causes) in October 1872. Long before he died, however, a battle over who would succeed him as Zulu king had begun. Mpande intended his son Mbuyazi to be his successor. But Mbuyazi's half brother Cetshwayo had a greater following among the Zulu people. The two princes arranged a hunt as a contest to decide the issue. Both princes gathered thousands of armed "hunters" as the hunt turned into war. Cetshwayo had a far larger army, whose fighters were called uSuthu on account of their battle cry, "uSuthu!" "Suthu" were a type of cattle that Cetshwayo's men had captured in an earlier battle. The cry of "uSuthu" kept alive the memory of these warriors' bravery during that battle. But Mbuyazi had some white fighters from Natal on his side. Armed with better guns and better trained to use them, these Natalians posed a serious threat in spite of their small number. They included John Dunn, a white trader and adventurer who lived as a Zulu chief in Natal. (Shaka appointed several of the original white Natal settlers as Zulu chiefs, and

A HAND-COLORED LANTERN SLIDE FROM THE NINETEENTH CENTURY
DEPICTS THE ZULU KING CETSHWAYO IN 1878.

some adopted Zulu lifestyles. They married several Zulu women and
lived in *kraals*. These complexes of huts surrounded a cattle enclosure
and were the nineteenth-century Zulu family settlements.)

In the end, Cetshwayo defeated Mbuyazi. Cetshwayo's forces
chased John Dunn's men to the swollen Inyoni River, where they

THE AFTERMATH OF THE ANGLO-ZULU WAR

escaped on boats. From then on, Mpande reigned in name only, and Cetshwayo acted as head of the Zulu nation.

Upon Mpande's death in 1872, a mourning period began. It lasted for about nine months. In July 1873, with the mourning period ended, Cetshwayo went to Ulundi for the ceremony that formally made him king. In accordance with the custom of the Zulu royal family, Cetshwayo was declared king by Mpande's head *induna* (minister), Masiphula, in a series of ceremonies. The guests included prominent figures from other Zulu groups. Among them were the induna Mnyamana, leader of the Buthelezi; the great general Zibhebhu, leader of the Mandlakazi; and Hamu, leader of the Ngenetsheni.

Like his father, Cetshwayo drew upon support from Natal, hoping that British-ruled Natal would assist him against Boer land claims. To demonstrate his friendship with Natal and the British Empire, he had invited the British secretary for native affairs at Natal, Theophilus Shepstone, to attend the Ulundi ceremony. (In the late 1800s, the British Empire—one of the world's most powerful—ruled a number of colonies around the globe.)

On August 1, 1873, following the Zulu ceremony, Shepstone held another coronation ceremony and himself crowned Cetshwayo king.

As British secretary for native affairs in Natal, Theophilus Shepstone, below, crowned Cetshwayo Zulu King and promised a commission to investigate Boer encroachment on Zulu lands.

Early Nineteenth-Century Zulu Culture

AT THE BEGINNING OF the nineteenth century, a small group of people known as the Zulu lived to the north of the Tugela River in southeastern Africa. The region had a mild climate and plentiful rainfall during the yearly rainy season, both of which supported the Zulu lifestyle as farmers and cattle herders. Zulu women did much of the work of the household. They raised crops, especially sorghum and corn. They hauled water for the gardens and for household use. They prepared food and the sour milk and sorghum beer that were staples of the Zulu diet. Zulu boys tended and milked the cattle, which were a primary source of food. Cattle also represented the wealth of the household and were used as a form of currency. Zulu men kept track of the cattle and maintained the cattle enclosures and huts. Men had responsibility for defense. The Zulu society also contained specialists, such as the men who worked iron to produce tools and weapons and the doctors who used a wide range of herbs to care for the sick and injured. The Zulu also relied on *angomas,* people who dealt with ancestral spirits and were called upon to "smell out" witches when people believed they had been wronged through evil-intentioned magic spells.

Just as cattle held a central position in the Zulu way of life, the cattle enclosure occupied the center of the homestead. Zulu huts surrounded the enclosure, forming a compound called a kraal. A central hut housed the main wife of the male head of the household, whose son would be his heir. Zulu men generally married more than one woman if they could afford the *lobolo* (cattle given to the bride's family as payment for the loss of the daughter's labor). Each wife lived in her own additional hut. Another hut was for his daughters, another for sons who had not yet grown up and established their own households, and still other huts for storing food. If the man was wealthy and influential, he also had additional huts for his followers.

"The huts are of a compact wicker work, circular in form, and much in the shape of a beehive," wrote Charles Rowden Maclean, one of the first European visitors to Zulu lands, "averaging from ten to twenty feet [3 to 6 meters] in diameter. . . . They are very neatly covered with thatch of a long tough grass, and the floor, composed of a mixture of mingled clay and cowdung, is of a glossy smoothness, having even a bright polish." A fire was kept burning in the center of the hut, Maclean wrote, so that a "dense cloud of smoke floating within a foot or two of the floor . . . renders it impossible to sit up." People entered the huts by crawling through a doorway about 18 inches (45.7 centimeters) high.

At the coronation, Shepstone promised to create a commission to investigate Zulu complaints about Boer encroachment.

Shepstone's crowning of Cetshwayo suggested British authority in Zululand: "Here is your king," Shepstone declared before the entire Zulu army and all the chiefs gathered for the coronation. "*You* have recognized him as such, and I now do so also, in the name of the Queen of England. Your kings have often met violent deaths by the hand of your own people, and if you kill this one, we shall require his blood at your hands." Thus it appeared that, although Cetshwayo was king of Zululand, he was subordinate to the Queen of England.

Cetshwayo made a number of promises to Shepstone in return for British support of his monarchy. A few of the promises benefited Cetshwayo. For instance, Cetshwayo promised that no one in Zululand would be sentenced to die without the king's consent. Before this time, the Zulu chiefs as well as the Zulu king held the power of life and death over their subjects. Now such decisions rested solely with the king. Other promises, though, limited the king's royal power. For instance, Cetshwayo could no longer declare war without British permission. Nevertheless, he accepted the restrictions and limitations on his authority. In return, he hoped for British help in stemming the advance of Boer settlers into his kingdom. With British recognition of the legitimacy of the Zulu king, he hoped that the Boer advance would be stopped at Utrecht. Cetshwayo also hoped the Boers would be forced to stand by their 1842 agreement with Mpande.

COLONIAL AFFAIRS AND BORDER ISSUES

Ignoring the 1842 agreement with Mpande, Boers had continued to settle east and north of Utrecht. Throughout the early years of Cetshwayo's reign, accusations of cattle and horse theft volleyed between

Zulu and Boer residents. These charges were commonly heard along the border and in the disputed territories claimed by Boers in the 1840s. Zulu messengers repeatedly traveled to the British colonial government headquarters in Natal asking them to help solve the problems. The Boers also complained to Shepstone about the border issues. But nothing came of the Zulu requests or Boer complaints. The promised commission, for the time being, remained merely a promise.

In the meantime, major changes were under way that deeply affected British policy and actions in Zululand. In 1877, Shepstone became heavily involved in negotiations with the Boer republic in the Transvaal. As a result of the negotiations, the Transvaal became a British colony and Shepstone became its administrator. He understood that, were he to be able to solve the territorial claims in Zululand in the Boers' favor, he would be able to expand his Transvaal colony.

In the same year, the British government appointed a high commissioner for all the British colonies in southern Africa, including Cape Colony, Natal, and the Transvaal. The high commissioner would also hold the position of commander in chief of all British armed forces there. For high commissioner, the British government chose Sir Henry Bartle Edward Frere, the new governor of Britain's oldest colony in southern Africa, Cape Colony. Frere saw an independent Zululand as a threat to the security of the colonies under his control. He believed that Zululand should be firmly under British control. This, he thought, could only be done by military action, an opinion that Shepstone came to share. Frere misled leaders back home about the situation in Zululand in hope of drawing Britain into a war to establish dominance over Zululand. He made sure that Zululand was portrayed in Great Britain as a land of "grinding despotism [unlimited power]" under a "cruel sovereign." He also claimed that Cetshwayo had broken the promises made at his coronation. This claim was highly exaggerated at best.

Cetshwayo's Broken Promises

ALTHOUGH FRERE MADE much of Cetshwayo's supposed violation of his coronation promises to Shepstone, the promises actually held no legal weight. As the secretary of state for the colonies, Lord Kimberley later said to the House of Lords [the upper house of the British Parliament, or legislative body], "The fact was that these were friendly assurances, given in response to friendly advice, . . . constituted no engagement."

Of the broken promises themselves, Frere made several claims. Most of the claims had to do with Cetshwayo's preparation to attack Natal or the Transvaal without British permission. Another claim was that Cetshwayo had hurriedly executed hundreds of people without trial. Later, a few executions under Cetshwayo's rule were confirmed, but all fell short of the actions described by Frere.

FRICTION GROWS

In 1878 several events added to the friction between the Zulu kingdom and the nearby British colonies. One of the most notable of these occurred when the sons of Sihayo, a Zulu chief, went to Natal to recover two of Sihayo's wives. The two women had fled to Natal for safety after it was discovered that they had been unfaithful to their husband. Sihayo's sons killed the women (death was the punishment for such behavior under Zulu law).

British authorities felt that once in Natal, the women should have been dealt with under British colonial law. They demanded that Sihayo's sons be turned over to British authorities in Natal, but Sihayo refused. Cetshwayo acknowledged that Sihayo's sons had acted improperly and that Sihayo was also at fault for not turning them over. However, he did not force Sihayo, one of his favorite chiefs, to hand over his sons to the British.

That same year, Sir Henry Bulwer, the British lieutenant governor of Natal, finally responded to the repeated Zulu requests for help with Boers settling on Zulu land. Bulwer appointed three commissioners to investigate both the Boer and the Zulu claims. The commissioners eventually decided that the Zulu claims were stronger. They agreed that Boers had unlawfully colonized the disputed land. The commissioners promised to report this decision to Shepstone. The commission found these Boers' blatant disregard for Zulu territorial rights so shocking that they praised the "self-restraint and moderation of the Zulus in reference to the much vexed boundary question." However, Shepstone had to consider the desires of the Boers of the Transvaal, who were under his charge. The Transvaal Boers supported the land claims of the Boers in Zululand. Shepstone hesitated to settle the boundary question immediately, promising a decision later.

MORE TENSION

Since High Commissioner Frere's arrival in southern Africa, rumors had spread in Natal and Zululand that Britain intended to annex (take over) Zululand and that war was coming. Shepstone's delay on the Boer-Zulu land dispute, along with the presence of British forces in Natal and the Transvaal, fueled the rumors. British troop movements along both sides of Zululand's borders with Natal and the Transvaal added to the tension. Cetshwayo grew increasingly suspicious of British intentions.

At the same time, a faction (group) intent on going to war was developing among the younger Zulu warriors. Young warriors who had been raised in the military culture established by Shaka, yet who had not experienced military action, "were getting very restless and quarrelsome," Cetshwayo reported. They were "anxious to get a chance of 'washing' their spears. They were intent on having a war somewhere, and proposed a raid into Swaziland [the Swazi kingdom to the north of Zululand] solely for this purpose." War provided a means for warriors to increase their wealth through seizing enemy cattle and being rewarded in cattle by their king for acts of bravery. It could thus provide a way for young men to accumulate cattle for lobolo (cattle given to the bride's family as payment for the loss of the daughter's labor) that would enable them to marry.

Earlier Zulu kings had fought the Swazi many times, creating unfriendly relations between the two peoples. Border raids occurred often. Cetshwayo considered declaring war on the Swazi to relieve his young warriors' tensions. He did not want to risk the possibility of his anxious young warriors attacking the British troops on the border and getting him involved in an all-out war with British forces. Cetshwayo therefore requested permission from the British to declare war on the Swazi. This permission was denied, and rather than break his coronation promise to the British, Cetshwayo disbanded his army. The young Zulu warriors, however, began to stir up anti-British feelings. They claimed that the British were behaving suspiciously. Older and wiser figures, including the king's ministers Hamu, Mnyamana, and Zibhebhu, urged caution. Cetshwayo followed their advice.

An Ultimatum

Young Zulu warriors were not the only ones intent on war. Powerful administrators in the British colonies of southern Africa supported High Commissioner Frere's ideas of going to war to subdue Zululand. They considered this a necessary step for the security of the British colonies in southern Africa, so they found a way of pushing tensions to a head. Frere and his supporters came up with an ultimatum. British delegates (representatives) led by John Shepstone, Theophilus Shepstone's younger brother and acting secretary for native affairs since 1876, presented the terms of the ultimatum to a delegation of several Zulu chiefs (which did not include Cetshwayo) on December 11, 1878. The demands of the ultimatum included a requirement that Cetshwayo turn over Sihayo's sons along with five hundred cattle as a fine for the Sihayo affair. (Zulu wealth at the time was measured in terms of cattle.) He was also to turn over an additional one hundred cattle as a fine for an earlier event known as the Middle Drift affair, in which armed Zulu men had prevented British workers from completing a road from Natal into Zululand. The ultimatum did not stop with these demands. The buthos, or all of Cetshwayo's regiments, were to be disbanded. The Zulu nation was to completely disarm, leaving itself defenseless. Finally, if Cetshwayo did not meet all of the demands within thirty days, the British would invade Zululand. (A government representative in London later rebuked Frere for issuing this ultimatum and for misusing British troops, sent to Natal for defense, in waging an offensive war. But by the time the events in Zululand came to light in Great Britain, it was too late.)

CETSHWAYO'S REACTION

Outraged, the members of the Zulu delegation did not want to convey the terms of the ultimatum to Cetshwayo. This reluctance, along with rains and flooded streams that slowed the delegation's progress, resulted in a long delay before the chiefs reported back to Cetshwayo. When the chiefs at last arrived, they told Cetshwayo only about certain portions of Shepstone's demands. At first, Cetshwayo thought that he was being asked to pay one hundred cattle for the Middle Drift affair and to turn over five hundred cattle *in the place of* Sihayo's sons. If this was all that was needed to please the British, Ceshwayo was happy to comply. He sent a message to the British saying that he was rounding up the six hundred cattle.

The message was received by Lieutenant General Frederic Augustus Thesiger Chelmsford, who had been put in charge of the British forces that were readying to invade Zululand from Natal and the Transvaal as soon as the thirty days set by the ultimatum expired. Chelmsford replied that nothing short of meeting *all* of the conditions would prevent the British troops from entering Zululand. He said that Cetshwayo must turn over Sihayo's sons as well as the cattle and completely disarm within the original thirty days.

To avoid war, Cetshwayo wanted to meet at least some of the demands, such as paying the cattle fines. However, his younger warriors refused to let him make concessions. They turned back a herd of about six hundred cattle that Cetshwayo had sent toward Natal, and they refused to send Sihayo's sons.

As for the demand that Cetshwayo disband his armies, he refused. Hoping to buy time, he continued to send messages to the British. He stated that he wanted to avoid war with the British and that he would send cattle to pay the fines. He also made a token effort to capture Sihayo's sons, but they escaped. Cetshwayo sent a message to report their escape to Chelmsford. By the time the messenger reached Chelmsford, however, "the English troops had entered Zululand, shots had been exchanged, and the two nations were at war."

With the approach of January 10, 1879, the thirtieth day of the ultimatum, Cetshwayo ordered his troops to prepare for war. Altogether, he was able to muster more than thirty thousand men.

While he was preparing to defend Zululand, Cetshwayo decided he would not attack the British forces first or invade Natal. Instead, he planned to gather his forces at Ulundi "to force the English to march up to where he was." Fearing the outcome, Dunn had urged Cetshwayo not to fight the British. When Cetshwayo ignored his advice, Dunn turned his back on his one-time friend and took two thousand of his followers and three thousand cattle into Natal.

FAST FACT

THE JANUARY 10, 1879, ULTIMATUM DEADLINE COINCIDENTALLY FELL TWO DAYS LATER THAN THE UMKHOSI HARVEST FESTIVAL. SINCE ALL OF HIS REGIMENTS WERE GATHERED TOGETHER FOR THE FESTIVAL, CETSHWAYO ORDERED THEM TO PREPARE FOR WAR INSTEAD OF THE FESTIVAL.

THE INVASION BEGINS

On January 11, 1879, thirty days after Shepstone issued Frere's ultimatum, Chelmsford's forces crossed the Buffalo River into Zulu territory at Rorke's Drift. The invading forces included more than fifteen thousand British, colonial, and African fighters. They were divided into five columns (units), spread out so that the Zulu troops would have little chance to get behind them and launch a counterinvasion of Natal.

The next day, the march passed through Sihayo's territory and near his homestead of Sokhexe. Chelmsford sent a portion of the column against Sokhexe, although Sihayo himself was away with the Zulu army. At Sokhexe the British encountered only a few defenders, most of whom fled after a brief fight. During this fight, sixteen of the Zulu defenders were killed. One of them was Sihayo's son Nkumikazulu, one of the men demanded by the British ultimatum. After the fight, the troops burned Sokhexe down.

Cetshwayo kept a number of his soldiers in reserve at Ulundi. But on January 17 and 18, he sent out three armies, one for each of the main British columns. He told them not to invade Natal but only to defend Zululand. He also asked his generals to try to negotiate once

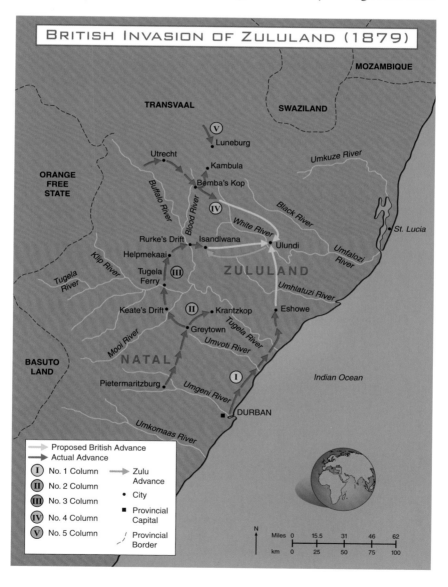

BRITISH INVASION OF ZULULAND (1879)

MOZAMBIQUE

TRANSVAAL

SWAZILAND

Ⓥ Luneburg

Utrecht

Umkuze River

Kambula

ORANGE
FREE
STATE

Bemba's Kop

Buffalo River

Blood River

Ⓘⓥ

White River

Black River

St. Lucia

Rurke's Drift

Isandlwana

Ulundi

Umfalozi River

Helpmekaai

ZULULAND

Klip River

Tugela
Ferry

Ⓘ Ⓘ Ⓘ

Umhlatuzi River

Tugela
River

Keate's Drift

Ⓘ Ⓘ

Krantzkop

Eshowe

Greytown

Tugela River

Mool River

Umvoti River

BASUTO
LAND

NATAL

Ⓘ

Indian Ocean

Pietermaritzburg

Umgeni River

DURBAN

Umkomaas River

Proposed British Advance
Actual Advance

Ⓘ No. 1 Column
Ⓘ No. 2 Column
Ⓘ No. 3 Column
Ⓘⓥ No. 4 Column
Ⓥ No. 5 Column

Zulu
Advance

City

Provincial
Capital

Provincial
Border

N

Miles 0   15.5   31   46   62
km   0   25   50   75   100

again with the British before engaging in battle. Beyond that, said Cetshwayo, "They had orders to drive back the columns, and were not hampered with any particular instructions, but were left to act independently as they thought best."

THE BATTLE AT ISANDHLWANA

The Zulu and British columns met at the Isandhlwana hill, about 10 miles (16 km) into Zululand from Rorke's Drift. The main Zulu army of more than twenty thousand men was commanded by Chief Ntshingwayo. He was about seventy years old and was a respected induna and warrior. The army camped in a nearby valley on the night of January 21. At the same time, the strongest of the British columns, the center column, was camped on the plain beneath the Isandhlwana hill. The Zulu warriors, hidden in the valley and taking care to light no fires, were invisible to the British. But the Zulu leaders knew where the British camp was because they had sent scouts ahead on horseback.

On January 21, British forces encountered about two thousand members of the Zulu army. Thinking they had discovered the main Zulu army, the British called for reinforcements. When these messengers reached Chelmsford at Isandhlwana that night, he decided to go to their aid before dawn. Chelmsford took with him most of the rest of the mounted men and all but two of the large six-pounder (2.7 kg) guns.

About seventeen hundred British soldiers remained at the camp at Isandhlwana. They had few horses and lacked most of their large guns. Even more fatefully, Chelmsford ignored the advice of experienced Boer fighters and left the camp unprotected. He had ordered neither laagering (drawing wagons into a circle that could be easily defended by riflemen) nor digging defensive trenches. The heavy ox-drawn wagons were difficult to move, digging in the rocky plain was slow work, and the Zulu armies were thought to be too far away to make the defensive efforts worthwhile.

Around noon on January 22, a small group of mounted British soldiers discovered the Zulu main army, which forced the Zulu warriors to attack earlier than their generals had planned. Not only had Cetshwayo commanded his officers not to be the first to attack, but January 22 was also the day of a new moon. A Zulu belief of the time considered the new moon to be an unlucky time for battle.

Nevertheless, if the Zulu army missed this opportunity to attack, they would lose their element of surprise. Even before the Zulu general could attempt to negotiate with the British, anxious warriors began heading into battle. Soon the Zulu army encircled the camp that Chelmsford had left behind at Isandhlwana. However, few of the Zulu guns had much effect because they were poorly aimed and it was difficult to see through the smoke from the British guns. The Zulu warriors were often able to avoid the cannon fire by dropping to the ground as the cannons were being fired and to avoid rifle fire by crawling toward the camp when the fire was heavy. Even so, hundreds of Zulu attackers were killed.

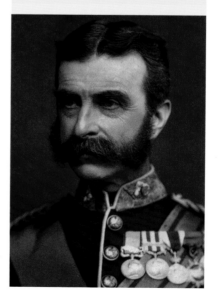

LIEUTENANT GENERAL FREDERIC CHELMSFORD WAS PUT IN CHARGE OF BRITISH FORCES PREPARING TO INVADE ZULULAND FROM NATAL AND THE TRANSVAAL.

In spite of their losses, the Zulu forces continued to advance. The British troops began to run short of ammunition, and their fire was reduced because of the need to stop and collect new cartridges. At that point, the Zulu warriors pressed in with their assegais, or iron-tipped spears, and devastated the British forces when they succeeded in getting close enough for hand-to-hand combat. Altogether, more than twelve hundred British troops were killed. Only a few escaped to cross a drift (an area of shallow water) on the Buffalo River back into Natal. Because of the rough terrain, even the few British soldiers who had horses could flee no faster than Zulu warriors could pursue them on foot. Zulu soldiers easily fired upon them as they crossed the drift.

On the one hand, the Zulu army had achieved a great victory at Isandhlwana. Their army had fought with spears and shields and old, inaccurate firearms. They had defeated a well-armed European army, killed nearly all of the British soldiers at the battle, and captured rifles and artillery. On the other hand, the victory was costly. "The army that had fought at Isandhlwana had lost very heavily," Cetshwayo lamented later. "They buried a large number of their dead. It was ten days before they returned to Ulundi, and then the *Indunas*, and quite a small part of the army, was all that appeared; most had gone to their homes with their wounded or their plunder . . . one regiment had lost over 500 men at Isandhlwana." In total, more than a thousand Zulu fighters were killed at Isandhlwana.

THE INVASION CONTINUES

The British defeat at Isandhlwana did not have the expected result of deterring the British from further conflict or of boosting Zulu morale. If anything, it steeled the determination of the British columns and forced them to regroup. And the victorious Zulu warriors became increasingly disheartened after seeing so much loss of life.

THE AFTERMATH OF THE ANGLO-ZULU WAR

CHARLES EDWIN FRIPP'S NINETEENTH-CENTURY OIL PAINTING DEPICTS A
SCENE FROM THE ZULU DEFEAT OF BRITISH FORCES AT THE BATTLE OF
ISANDHLWANA ON JANUARY 22, 1879.

The other British columns met with greater success than the center column did at Isandhlwana. Zulu general Godide's army, which had been sent against the British right column, was quickly defeated. Two days later, a patrol sent by Colonel Henry Evelyn Wood, who commanded the left column, surprised and defeated about three thousand Zulu warriors and their allies. Cetshwayo heard only later that they "had been defeated, and had scattered and gone to their homes."

Zulu forces met with a few more successes. In February and March of 1879, they surrounded Eshowe, where one of the main British columns had gathered, and managed to prevent an attack. Despite a few successful engagements, though, most of the encounters with the British led to Zulu defeats. Rather than fighting in the

The Defense of Rorke's Drift

ONE OF THE MOST famous British stories of the Anglo-Zulu War is that of the defense of Rorke's Drift. The attack took place on the Natal side of the Buffalo River at Rorke's Drift on January 22, 1879. There, a small garrison (group of people stationed at a military base) of eighty soldiers and thirty-five sick men were left to defend a supply depot and hospital after Lieutenant General Chelmsford crossed into Zululand.

A Zulu army of about 4,000 men attacked the garrison on January 22. The British soldiers had been warned of the attack by riders who had escaped the battle at Isandhlwana. Thanks to the warning, the garrison managed to defend themselves until reinforcements arrived the next morning. They killed between 370 and 600 Zulu warriors and lost only seventeen British soldiers.

THE BRITISH DEFENSE OF RORKE'S DRIFT IS DEPICTED IN ALPHONSE MARIE NEUVILLE'S 1880 OIL PAINTING.

open, the British used their superior firepower to defend fortified positions. Cetshwayo's battle plans took this British advantage into account, but his orders were not always carried out, leading to heavy losses.

THE AFTERMATH OF THE ANGLO-ZULU WAR

Cetshwayo repeatedly pleaded for peace, knowing that his forces could not win. He sent emissaries (representatives) and offerings of ivory and cattle to Chelmsford to try to negotiate. He even sent two British cannons captured at Isandhlwana. However, his young warriors preferred to keep fighting. They drove some of the cattle back to Ulundi and prevented the guns from being taken to Chelmsford. Furthermore, Chelmsford would accept nothing short of the terms laid out in the ultimatum. Meanwhile, British reinforcements had arrived at Natal, and Chelmsford was able to pull together his armies. Seeing no other course open to him, in June and July of 1879, Cetshwayo gathered his men together and moved toward Ulundi to meet Chelmsford.

THE BATTLE OF ULUNDI

On the morning of July 4, 1879, about twenty thousand warriors of the Zulu army were gathered near Ulundi. Cetshwayo himself had gone away to his royal homestead at uMbonambi to await the outcome of the battle. More than five thousand British soldiers drew up into a square formation, with their supplies, medical personnel, and reserves inside the square. Infantry (foot soldiers) formed the perimeter (outer limits) of the square. Marching in formation, they reached the chosen site for the battle, an exposed knoll raised slightly above the surrounding plain, before the Zulu army reached them. The cavalry (soldiers on horseback) remained outside the square at the beginning of the battle. They set fire to Zulu structures and engaged the Zulu warriors, attempting to draw them closer. The British forces wanted to bring the warriors within range of the infantry's rifles, the twelve pieces of artillery, and the two Gatling guns inside the square.

Cetshwayo's orders throughout the war required that the Zulu army avoid engaging a fortified British position. As at Eshowe, such positions were to be monitored closely and kept under threat of attack, but not attacked directly. But here the British stood in an open plain, and the moment for attack seemed to have arrived. But the cavalry on the square's perimeter proved fatal.

Although the Zulu fighters brought more guns to the battle of Ulundi than to any earlier battles involving Zulu forces, their shots had little effect. The disciplined firing of the British soldiers prevented the Zulu warriors from getting close enough to attack hand-to-hand. Not even the normally effective Zulu technique of crawling toward their enemies through the tall grass, so that enemies could not take aim effectively before the Zulu warriors leaped up and attacked, helped the Zulu cause.

The British lost only twelve men that day, and only sixty-nine were wounded. The Zulu lost at least five hundred or six hundred men during the attack on the British formation. Hundreds more

BRITISH FIREPOWER PROVED DECISIVE AGAINST REPEATED CHARGES BY ZULU WARRIORS DURING THE BATTLE OF ULUNDI. THIS PAINTING WAS DONE BY JAMES EDWIN MCDONNELL IN THE EARLY TWENTIETH CENTURY.

were killed while trying to flee or while attempting to regroup in the hills. Altogether, the number of Zulu losses probably totaled around fifteen hundred.

The Zulu warriors who escaped to the forest about 3 miles (5 km) away joined local residents who were fleeing with their cattle and belongings to the Bombo Mountains and to the Ngome forest. Cetshwayo issued orders for four of his regiments to regroup, but they refused. For all practical purposes, the Anglo-Zulu War was over, but its end brought neither effective British rule nor a halt to bloodshed in Zululand.

CHAPTER 2

The Aftermath: Surrender and Capture

WITH THE DEFEAT at the battle of Ulundi, Zulu resistance all but collapsed. The British victory bolstered colonists' confidence in Chelmsford and Frere. Within six months, the British had managed to soundly defeat the armies of the Zulu nation, which the British and Boer colonists had seen as a threat for nearly half a century. And they did so with relatively few British lives lost. They had even overseen the surrender of several important Zulu chiefs.

However, the government in Great Britain had been unsettled by the early defeats in the war, which it had not favored in the first place. Chelmsford received a telegram announcing a change of command:

> Her Majesty's Government have determined to send out Sir Garnet Wolseley as Administrator in that part of South-Eastern Africa in the neighbourhood of the seat of war, with plenary [absolute] powers, both civil and military. Sir Bartle Frere, instructed accordingly by Colonial Office. The ap-

pointment of a senior officer is not intended as a censure on [criticism of] yourself, but you will, as in ordinary course of service, submit and subordinate your plans to his control.

Although the telegram stated that the change was not intended as punishment for failure, it undoubtedly appeared so.

About a month after the decisive July 4, 1879, victory, Chelmsford began the withdrawal of his forces. Disheartened by the news in the telegram and continuing to regret the defeat at Isandhlwana, he was anxious to resign his command. "As I have fully accomplished the object for which I advanced," he wrote on the day of victory to the new British administrator, or high commissioner, of southeastern Africa, "I consider I shall now be best carrying out Sir Garnet Wolseley's instructions by moving at once to Entonjanini, and thence to Kwamagwaza [moving southwest through Zululand toward Natal]."

All across Zululand, the withdrawing British troops encountered no sign that the Zulu army was regrouping. They came across old men, women, and children, some driving herds of cattle or goats. They also saw Zulu warriors, resigned to their defeat, moving across the open country on their way home to their families. Sporadic violence continued, but the war between the Zulu and British armies was, for all purposes, over.

FAST FACT

A POWERFUL HAILSTORM THAT HALTED CHELMSFORD'S WITHDRAWAL FROM JULY 5 TO JULY 9, 1879, ALSO PREVENTED FRIENDS AND FAMILIES OF ZULU WARRIORS FALLEN AT THE BATTLE OF ULUNDI FROM REMOVING MORE THAN A FEW OF THE BODIES FROM THE SITE OF THE BATTLE. EVEN NINE MONTHS LATER, THE BONES OF THE DEFEATED LAY STREWN ACROSS THE PLAIN.

Garnet Wolseley and the Terms of Surrender

Even as Chelmsford's exhausted soldiers were withdrawing, the new high commissioner, Garnet Wolseley, raised two new columns to march through Zululand. He wanted to ensure that all the remaining Zulu chiefs surrendered. One column, led by Lieutenant Colonel C. M. Clarke and accompanied by Wolseley himself, proceeded back toward Ulundi. The other, led by Lieutenant Colonel Baker Russell, headed for northwestern Zululand. The terms of surrender that Wolseley offered were much more lenient than terms Zulu victors generally offered. For this reason, they seemed acceptable to many Zulu chiefs. Zulu warfare usually resulted in the killing of the defeated chief, either literally or by forcing him to give up power. Defeat also frequently meant that his group would be eaten up. This was the Zulu way of saying that the losing chief's cattle would all go to the victor, as would the women and children of his household.

Zulu chiefs surrender to Sir Garnet Wolseley at Emmangweni in August 1879.

Wolseley demanded that the Zulu chiefs turn over their guns and royal herds of cattle, that they formally surrender, and that they promise to cooperate with the British in the future. In return, the British agreed to not seize land or cattle belonging to the Zulu people. Chiefs who cooperated would retain their chieftainships.

Many of the chiefs, including the king's half brother Dabulamanzi, surrendered under these terms. In addition to the relatively mild terms of surrender, other factors led many of the chiefs to surrender. With the country in disarray, sowing and harvesting crops were impossible. A lengthy war would lead to starvation.

"Our war is not against the Zulu people, but against Ketshwayo [Cetshwayo], who has broken all his promises. We have no wish to rob the Zulu people of their property or their land. . . . The Queen [of England] is most anxious that the war in Natal should be finished."

—British high commissioner Garnet Wolseley, 1879

Even so, several of the powerful Zulu chiefs hesitated, and Wolseley readily threatened violence. A July 14, 1879, letter told the powerful chiefs Mnyamana, Sekethwayo, Ntshingwayo, Zibhebhu, and Mnqandi that "Sir Garnet Wolselely desires you to meet him as soon as possible at Emmangweni. If you do not come to meet him, you will be regarded as an enemy of the English. If you do come to meet him, you will be treated as a friend and your cattle secured to you." The letter went on to say that Wolseley did not want to fight the Zulu people. He urged the chiefs to meet him as requested so that the war could be ended. It further claimed that the British did not intend to annex any part of Zululand. However, it also threatened to call the Swazi, with whom the British had been negotiating, to "clear out the Ngome forest" where Zulu people loyal to Cetshwayo were hiding.

FLIGHT OF CETSHWAYO

While British troops knew where to find Cetshwayo's followers, they did not know where to find the king. When Cetshwayo heard about the defeat at Ulundi, he had set out northward on foot with his household, including his eleven-year-old son Dinuzulu. Along the way, Cetshwayo took shelter with the prominent Zulu chief Zibhebhu. Cetshwayo left Dinuzulu with Zibhebhu and continued to the kraal of Mnyamana, one of his indunas, located across the Black Umfolozi River.

At Mnyamana's kraal, Cetshwayo hoped to calm the British by sending them a herd of cattle before surrendering himself. He gathered about four hundred cattle and sent them to Wolseley at Ulundi with a delegation of chiefs led by Mnyamana. In addition to handing over the cattle, Mnyamana pleaded for the life of the defeated king.

From there, Cetshwayo continued northward to the kraal of his brother Ziwedu. At Ziwedu's kraal, Cetshwayo several times received demands from the British to surrender in person rather than send messengers. Cornelius Vijn, a Dutch trader who had observed the battle for Cetshwayo, joined the king at several points during his flight and recorded the king's reactions to these demands. According to Vijn, Cetshwayo "dared not venture to come in [to a British camp], lest he should be shot dead or carried over the sea to Robben Island."

Sihayo's Sons

ON JULY 28, 1878, several of Zulu chief Sihayo's sons had led a group of warriors into Natal and executed two of Sihayo's wives as punishment for adultery. When Sir Henry Bulwer found out about the killings, he demanded that four of Sihayo's sons be turned over to the British authorities at Natal. Sihayo would not give them up, and Cetshwayo did not force him to do so. As a result, they became one of the pretexts for the British invasion of Zululand.

One of the sons, Bekuzulu, was discovered to have an alibi, having been at Cetshwayo's kraal at the time of the raid into Natal. Another, Nkumikazulu, was killed in battle. A third, Tshekwana, may also have died in battle, or he may have escaped into hiding.

The remaining son, ringleader Mehlokazulu, was captured and held as a prisoner of war. When the British released other Zulu prisoners of war at the end of the war in 1879, Mehlokazulu was turned over to British authorities to stand trial. Unlike most other prisoners accused of crimes in Natal, Mehlokazulu was not allowed to have a lawyer to defend him. Even so, the British colonial court decided that he had not committed a crime that could be punished by British authorities. The court added that he could be tried and punished by the Zulu king for his role in the unlawful killings, but by the time he was tried, Cetshwayo had been deposed. Therefore, Mehlokazulu was allowed to go home unpunished.

MEHLOKAZULU, SECOND FROM LEFT, WAS WANTED BY BRITISH AUTHORITIES FOR KILLING TWO WOMEN. CETSHWAYO REFUSED TO TURN HIM OVER TO THE BRITISH, ALTHOUGH HE WAS EVENTUALLY CAPTURED.

Cetshwayo knew about Robben Island, an island used as a prison several miles off the southwestern coast of what is modern-day South Africa near Cape Town. Natal authorities had sent a well-known chief from the Natal colony into exile there after they accused him of rebellion.

With each new message, Cetshwayo feared even more for his life. One message from Dabulamanzi stated that the British intended to kill Cetshwayo and that he should not surrender before the cattle were handed over to Wolseley. A later message from John Dunn informed Cetshwayo that British patrols were being sent to capture him. Dunn warned that "the English are only looking for a very small pretext for attacking you."

In pursuit of the Zulu king, the British patrols burned kraals, took prisoners and cattle, and flogged (whipped) those who refused to cooperate. But they could not convince the Zulu people to tell them where Cetshwayo was hiding. An interpreter with one of the British patrols wrote: "Although I believed they would be true to their king, I never expected such devotion. Nothing would move

English Miles

ONE SOURCE OF MISCOMMUNICATION that slowed the British hunt for Cetshwayo was the different ways by which people involved in the search calculated distance. For example, the British patrols relied on the English mile as a standard of reference. But Cornelius Vijn, one of the most important European guides, estimated and reported distances using Dutch miles, which were about four times as long as English miles. The Zulu people that Vijn and the patrols questioned were not accustomed to estimating distances in miles at all. Instead, they refered to natural landmarks like streams and hills and to the kraals of people living in the area.

them. Neither the loss of their cattle, the fear of death, or the offering of large bribes, would make them false to their king."

Cetshwayo traveled up the Black Umfolozi River from kraal to kraal, with British patrols in pursuit. Finally, hearing that the British had arrived at the wagon drift of the Black Umfolozi, he abandoned the river for the Ngome forest. While hiding there, the locals reported a rumor that Mnyamana was helping the British to capture the king.

The group of chiefs led by Mnyamana arrived at Wolseley's camp on August 14, 1879. They brought the four hundred cattle gathered by Cetshwayo and a few hundred more gathered by Mnyamana at Cetshwayo's orders. At that meeting, Wolseley convinced Mnyamana that the king would be safe if he surrendered. He also convinced Mnyamana and the other chiefs to surrender on the terms Wolseley had laid out rather than return to Cetshwayo.

CAPTURE OF CETSHWAYO

Through threats and trickery, one of the patrols finally obtained information on Cetshwayo's whereabouts. The patrols captured three brothers who lived at a kraal that the patrol believed Cetshwayo had passed through. The brothers claimed to have no knowledge of the king's whereabouts, even when threatened with death. Finally, the patrol officers blindfolded one of the brothers and took him out of sight in the forest. They fired a rifle into the air and came back and told the other two brothers that they had shot him. They then blindfolded and separated the remaining two brothers, telling them that they would shoot one and then the other, as they had shot their brother, if they did not tell them where Cetshwayo was.

Finally, the brothers admitted that the king had stayed at their kraal the night before. The patrol resumed the chase and alerted other patrols to the king's location.

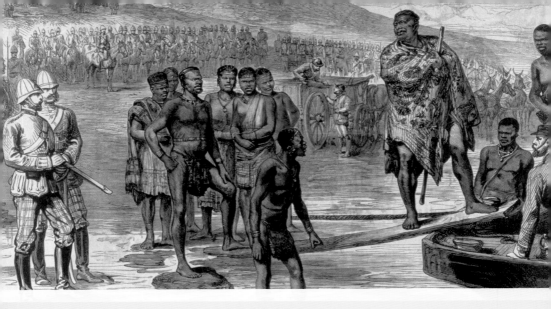

THE DEPOSED ZULU CHIEF CETSHWAYO, STANDING ON WOODEN PLANK, RIGHT, BOARDS A SMALL BOAT IN PORT DURNFORD FOR TRANSPORTATION INTO EXILE IN AUGUST 1879. THIS NINETEENTH-CENTURY WOOD ENGRAVING IS BY CRAWFORD CAFFIN.

The patrols finally caught up with and captured Cetshwayo in the Ngome forest on August 28, 1879. He was transported to the British camp at Ulundi, where he spent less than three hours. Wolseley did not even bother to meet him, a move that suggested that Wolseley considered him neither a defeated leader nor a deposed king, but a common prisoner of war.

From Ulundi, Cetshwayo was escorted to Port Durnford (on the east coast of what is modern-day South Africa) and then sent by steamboat to Cape Town, where he was imprisoned in an apartment in an old castle, which was usually referred to simply as "the Castle." The British had now not only defeated the Zulu military but also removed the king, the ultimate ruler, from Zululand. But what would they establish in his place?

CHAPTER 3

An Unworkable Settlement

I N THE AFTERMATH of the Anglo-Zulu War, Garnet Wolseley, the high commissioner for southeastern Africa, feared that the Zulu military would regroup under a new leader and that a newly unified Zulu nation would pose a threat to nearby British colonies. So Wolseley devised a plan to keep Zululand weak and its leaders loyal to Britain. This plan, Wolseley hoped, would provide a protective buffer around the colonies.

THE GATHERING AT ULUNDI

On September 1, 1879, Garnet Wolseley called a meeting of about two hundred Zulu chiefs. Wolseley's plan involved dividing the country into thirteen independent chiefdoms, each ruled by a chief of Wolseley's choosing. The chiefs would rule independently. This would ensure that no single ruler would gain too much power, which

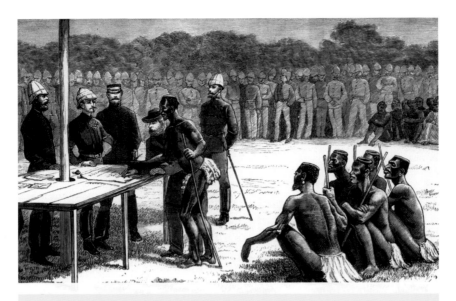

in turn would pose less of a threat to British interests in the region. British laws would not be forced upon the Zulu people, and Britain would not annex Zulu lands.

In exchange, the chiefs had to agree to certain terms. No executions could take place without trials, no chief would reestablish or maintain a standing army, and Zulu people would not be allowed to have guns or ammunition. In addition, a British resident, or magistrate (government administrative official and judge), would be brought in to settle disputes and to ensure that the chiefs did not stray from these rules. The magistrate would represent the British government in all matters.

THE THIRTEEN CHIEFDOMS

Wolseley chose the thirteen chiefs mainly from among leaders who had cooperated with the British or who could be expected to cooperate because of their ambition. Chiefs who had remained loyal to Cetshwayo would live in the lands of the thirteen new chiefs, subject to their rule. Even such important princes as Cetshwayo's brother Ndabuko, who was identified by one British official as "the man of greatest rank and influence in Zululand" now that the king was in exile, and Cetshwayo's son Dinuzulu were among those put under Zibhebhu, one of the thirteen British-appointed chiefs.

Wolseley offered Mnyamana an independent chieftainship in recognition of his timely surrender and his standing among the Zulu people. Mnyamana, however, refused, saying "My chiefship is dead. I was a chief in the Zulu country. I shall not now go and 'hold the feather' [sign treaties using a quill pen] of the white man's government, which has taken my chiefship away from me." The large tract of land over which he had formerly ruled was divided among three other chiefs.

Zulu loyalists were not alone in opposing Wolseley's plan. Some Natalian colonists also were skeptical of the plan. They feared it would lead to violence that would spill over into Natal. One other area of common concern involved Dunn. Dunn had advised Wolseley on how to divide Zululand and then was made chief of the large chiefdom bordering Natal. European colonists and Zulu loyalists both had harsh words for Dunn. They saw him as an opportunist, someone who would take advantage of events to serve his own best interests. In the process, Dunn had helped and harmed both sides. On the one hand, he was largely responsible for arming the Zulu military, and Cetshwayo's friendship had made Dunn's fortune possible. On the

BRITISH ADVENTURER JOHN DUNN BETRAYED HIS FRIENDSHIP WITH CETSHWAYO BY PROVIDING THE BRITISH GOVERNMENT WITH ARMS AND INFORMATION ABOUT THE ZULU.

other hand, Dunn had defected to the British and assisted them with both intelligence and arms. Now his treachery to the Zulu king was being rewarded by the British with the largest new independent chiefdom in Zululand.

In this situation, disputes were likely to occur. Yet the British resident had no practical power to enforce decisions, as no British forces were stationed in the chiefdoms. After just two months, the first appointee, William Wheelwright, gave the job up because, with no forces to back him up, he felt that he could not accomplish anything. The second resident, Melmoth Osborn, strongly believed in preventing a return of Zulu royal power in Zululand. So he used his influence to make sure that this did not occur.

ABUSES BY APPOINTED CHIEFS

Zulu factions soon began vying for power. In the absence of British troops and police, some of the newly appointed chiefs ignored their pledge and began arming their followers. Some of the disputes between Zulu factions turned ugly. During his flight, Cetshwayo had left his eleven-year-old son Dinuzulu in the care of Zibhebhu. He had also left

THE AFTERMATH OF THE ANGLO-ZULU WAR

the *ndlunkulu* (girls who had been presented to the king by subject chiefs and for whom he acted as "father," arranging their marriages), and large herds of his cattle with his former general. These people and property of the royal family remained in Zibhebhu's care when Zibhebhu became one of the thirteen appointed chiefs. However, Dinuzulu observed that in Cetshwayo's absence, Zibhebhu almost immediately began taking girls from the ndlunkulu and cattle from the royal herds for his own use. Seeing this, Dinuzulu ran away to join Mnyamana and his uncles. This group would become the center of a loyalist movement, whose supporters were called uSuthu (the same name used by Cetshwayo's supporters when he vied for the kingship in 1856). And they grew increasingly enraged at Zibhebhu for taking royal property.

Zibhebhu was not the only chief who used his position to take advantage of the defeated loyalists. Appointed chiefs Dunn and Hamu seized the private cattle of the uSuthu, claiming these people were hiding royal cattle and guns. Dunn formed his own army. And in July 1880, he allowed his men to slaughter more than two hundred people, including fleeing women and children, when he took sides in a dispute between some of the people in his chiefdom. Hamu, who had gone over to the British during the war, killed several of those who had opposed his defection.

Wolseley later expressed regret for having chosen Hamu as a chief. "Hamu is not a chief whom of my own choice I should have selected for rule in Zululand. But I had no option in regard to his appointment, for the British Government were under pledges made to him at the time of his defection from Cetshwayo by Colonel Wood and Lord Chelmsford."

THE uSUTHU RAISE CONCERNS

The uSuthu found these abuses intolerable. However, they had no power under the Wolseley settlement to fight back. The only solution, as they perceived it, was for the British to replace the problem chiefs with more honorable men such as Cetshwayo. They sent representatives, who walked hundreds of miles on several trips to and from Natal, to express these views.

The first of these visits took place in Pietermaritzburg, the capital of Natal, in February 1880. There the uSuthu representatives were told that the British authorities did not approve of cattle seizures or of appointed chiefs' mistreatment of their subjects. However, the proper arbiter (judge) of such matters, they were told, was Osborn, the British resident in Zululand. So the uSuthu representatives returned to Zululand, only to have Osborn tell them that he was not responsible for the behavior and relationships among the various Zulu chiefs and groups. His responsibility, he said, was to make sure that Wolseley's "laws" in Zululand were carried out. He issued the group a pass to present their case again in Pietermaritzburg. (The colonial government required that Zulu people living in Zululand had to have a pass signed by government authorities in order to cross the border into Natal.)

Twice more, the uSuthu traveled to Pietermaritzburg. The unsettled situation in Zululand had become so dangerous that even some of the appointed chiefs were beginning to protest. In the first of the two visits, in May 1880, the uSuthu group had said they were under the authority of other appointed chiefs as well as of uSuthu leaders. By the next visit, in July 1881, they claimed to have been sent under the authority of eight of the thirteen appointed chiefs as well as the two leaders of the uSuthu. Both times, the representatives presented their case to the British authorities, and both times they were referred to Osborn, who avoided seeing them and refused to deal with the issue.

Around the time of the delegation's 1881 visit to Pietermaritzburg, a British investigator, Sir Evelyn Wood, arrived in Zululand to look into the complaints against Hamu, Zibhebhu, and Dunn. His rulings did little to fix the tensions. He supported

Dunn's actions of July 1880, as Dunn claimed to be keeping order. Wood also pronounced that if the uSuthu princes left Zibhebhu's territory and went to Dunn's territory, Zibhebhu would be ordered to return a small proportion of their cattle—but only if they accepted Dunn's rule. Regarding Mnyamana's claims against Hamu, Wood stated that Hamu must return some of the cattle he had seized, but not all of them. He justified this decision to Mnyamana saying, "As for you, you have no voice here. You refused a chieftainship, we then told you to go to Hamu; you refused that also."

EVELYN WOOD WAS SENT TO ZULULAND BY THE BRITISH GOVERNMENT IN 1881 TO INVESTIGATE uSUTHU COMPLAINTS AGAINST SOME OF THE ZULU CHIEFS AND JOHN DUNN.

The uSuthu princes living in Zibhebhu's territory refused to submit to Dunn and took shelter with Mnyamana. When Osborn would not permit them to stay there, the women of the royal household, including twenty-five wives of Cetshwayo and the wives of Cetshwayo's brother Ndabuko, took matters into their own hands. They approached Osborn themselves, saying,

> Since you have taken us away from the King, it is you who ought to take care of us, you who are responsible for us. How should you give us to John Dunn? Is it fitting, when he was merely one of our indunas (officers). And do you now set on

Zibebu [Zibhebhu] and Hamu to destroy us? If you will not take charge of us yourself, give us a letter that we may go down to the authorities at [Pieter]Maritzburg. We will not belong to Zibebu [Zibhebhu], nor to Hamu, nor to John Dunn.

"All what is mine in Zululand has been overturned and spoiled. My children and wives have been put in misery by the chiefs now ruling, specially Dunn. The English were merciful, but not the chiefs now ruling."

—Cetshwayo, March 29, 1881

Osborn replied that he thought the women would have gone back to their fathers' kraals rather than to Mnyamana's. The idea shocked the women. In Zulu culture at that time, such a move was viewed as a dishonor. A married Zulu woman was sent back to live at her father's house only if she had committed a crime. Osborn compromised and allowed the women to stay at uSuthu kraals in another territory.

When the uSuthu delegation returned from Pietermaritzburg, Osborn listened to their complaints. However, he took Zibhebhu's and Hamu's side. Hamu interpreted this decision as approval to use force against supporters of the uSuthu. So he sent an army against the Qulusi, who lived in his territory but had strongly supported Cetshwayo and had refused to accept Hamu's authority. Hamu's army killed most of the fifteen hundred Qulusi soldiers, and the survivors fled across the river to the Transvaal.

Because of the scale of violence, unprecedented during Cetshwayo's rule, two more uSuthu delegations made their way to Natal to express their frustration to British officials. Neither delegation was successful in making its case, and Natal officials did not act against Zibhebhu, Hamu, or Dunn. Nor did either delegation convince the officials that Cetshwayo should be restored to power. However, in April 1882, a large delegation known as the Great Deputation headed for Natal from Zululand. The group included more than two thousand representatives, including 646 chiefs. Even some of the British-appointed chiefs sent representatives with the delegation. The scale of the protest suggested to the British government that the uSuthu cause had widespread support in Zululand. British authorities finally began to take note.

However, the authorities once again chose not to act. The members of the delegation hesitated to cross the border back into Zululand. They feared that, with Dunn, Hamu, and Zibhebhu receiving so much support from Osborn, they would meet armed opposition from the armies of those chiefs.

THE TRANSVAAL BOERS AND THE SOUTH AFRICAN REPUBLIC

The aftermath of the Anglo-Zulu War led to some benefits for the Boers of Transvaal. First of all, Wolseley's settlement gave them firm control of the territories in Zululand that they had long claimed. Furthermore, with conflicts over this territory ended, Boers in the Transvaal had more time to focus on their ultimate goal—independence from British rule. They began pushing for this change when, in December 1880, a Boer farmer in the Transvaal refused to pay taxes to the British. This act of rebellion quickly led to the mobilization (arming) of Boer commandos (military units). Over the next few months, Boers attacked British forces throughout the Transvaal. All of the besieged garrisons (military posts) held out. However, the British were defeated in a number of skirmishes, so the British government decided to withdraw from the Transvaal. As part of the peace agreement negotiated in 1881, the British again recognized the Transvaal's right to self-government as the newly independent South African Republic. However, the treaty included an ambiguous phrase that Britain later used to claim that it had not granted complete independence.

The violence on the republic's borders—most notably, the slaughter of the Qulusi—worried the Transvaalers. They thought that Zulu groups in Zululand had been less violent under Cetshwayo's rule. In fact, in a message to the British, the Transvaalers made it clear that they were "soliciting Cetshwayo's release and restoration, as an act of justice, and to prevent bloodshed." His release, they felt, would calm the Zulu nation and lead to peace.

CETSHWAYO IN CAPE TOWN

Although the British confined Cetshwayo to his apartments in the Castle in Cape Town between 1879 and 1881, he became something of a celebrity in Cape Town. Many people, from idle gawkers to high society, thronged to the Castle, hoping to meet the deposed king who had once defeated a modern British army. During this time, Cetshwayo began to learn British customs, believing this to be a way to better present his case to British authorities. For example, he adopted a British style of dressing, including suits and hats, so that Europeans would view him as dignified.

Cetshwayo refused to become a mere showpiece, however, admitting only those visitors he viewed as worthy of his royal dignity.

He refused to see the curious masses who thronged to the Castle. Although his "guests" to the apartments had to be approved, the British authorities usually approved requests from high-ranking visitors. Cetshwayo could also request meetings in the Castle. He chose

A WOODCUT FROM THE 1800S DEPICTS CETSHWAYO'S 1879 ARRIVAL IN CAPE TOWN, WHERE HE SPENT TWO YEARS IN EXILE.

these meetings carefully, mostly seeing powerful politicians and distinguished public figures who could someday provide valuable help. His guests at the castle included Prince George and Prince Albert from Great Britain, who carried their good impression of the former king back to Queen Victoria. When Cetshwayo was alone, he practiced writing, for like most Zulu people of his day, he was illiterate.

In February 1881, Cetshwayo was moved to a farm called Oude Molen, a few miles from Cape Town. He had considerable freedom to move about compared to the confinement of the Castle, and he was permitted to keep cattle and to hunt. But Oude Molen's distance from the convenient transportation and communications facilities of Cape Town made it difficult for visitors to come. What Cetshwayo truly desired, more than greater freedom of movement or leisure activities, was to make a trip to England to plead his case before the British authorities there and to be restored to Zululand. Toward this end, he dictated dozens of letters which were sent to important and powerful people including Sir Hercules Robinson, the British governor of Cape Colony; William Ewart Gladstone, the British prime

WHILE IN EXILE AT CAPE TOWN, CETSHWAYO ABANDONED HIS TRADITIONAL ZULU CLOTHING IN FAVOR OF SUITS AND HATS. HE HOPED THE EUROPEANS WOULD SEE THIS CHANGE AS A SIGN OF HIS DIGNITY.

THE AFTERMATH OF THE ANGLO-ZULU WAR

minister; Lord Kimberley, who was in charge of the Colonial Office in London; and Queen Victoria.

THE BRITISH POLITICAL CLIMATE

In Great Britain, the ruling political party and much of public opinion had come to consider the Anglo-Zulu war to have been misguided. Before the war, Frere and his allies had convinced the British public that the Zulu people would welcome the British as liberators if they deposed Cetshwayo. The British were dismayed that this had not occurred. In addition, Cetshwayo's letters from Oude Molen won a certain amount of sympathy from leading British political figures, including Queen Victoria. Some of these leaders came to realize that Frere had misled them. They also started to suspect that the Wolseley settlement might not be in Britain's best interests.

The British were also influenced by news of the unrest in Zulu-land. Osborn had helped delay that news but it had finally started trickling back to London. There, people were astonished to learn of the level of support for the uSuthu cause, as demonstrated by the number and status of the chiefs who had marched to Pieter-maritzburg in the Great Deputation. News of the first deputation to Pietermaritzburg, in February 1880, had not even reached the British prime minister's office until February 1881. But as that year progressed, government officials in London began to seriously con-sider that the calls for Cetshwayo's return might be genuine and that he might help stabilize Zululand and thereby, southeast Africa.

CETSHWAYO DEPARTS FOR ENGLAND

At last Cetshwayo received word that his outreach to the British was beginning to bear fruit. "Inform Cetshwayo that his wishes have been considered, but a visit to England at approach of winter is for various reasons very undesirable," read a September 14, 1881, telegram from the Home Government (the British government in London, which had ultimate authority over British colonies) to the British authorities in the Cape Colony. It continued: "Besides the danger to his health, many things interesting to him cannot be seen at that season. He must leave it to Her Majesty's Government to determine when it will be best for him to come." Another reason for the delay was that the British government had not yet decided what Cetshwayo's fate would be. Reinstalling him as Zulu king was an option, but so was continued exile. The British worried that an immediate trip to England would seem a sign that Cetshwayo was to be returned to Zululand as king. Some feared that he might commit suicide (he had already talked about doing so) if he went to England and then had to remain in exile. Therefore, the British authorities concluded that Cetshwayo should not be invited to London until his reinstallation as king was a real likelihood.

Cetshwayo's visit to England was delayed for other reasons as well. The Governor of Natal, Henry Bulwer, reported growing unrest among the people of Zululand as word of Cetshwayo's possible visit to England spread. Lord Kimberley, the colonial secretary in London, received from Bulwer a warning that "the intended visit of Cetshwayo to England had led to the report of his restoration, and was used to create agitation." Bulwer insisted that Cetshwayo be delayed in setting out for England until the "agitation" was resolved. Bulwer's messages gave the impression that the Zulu people were unsettled because of widespread opposition to Cetshwayo's return to Zululand.

Upon investigation, though, Kimberley discovered that the "agitation" actually referred to the Great Deputation. The unrest was caused by those who wanted the king restored, so delaying Cetshwayo's visit to England would only prolong the unrest. Kimberley

THE AFTERMATH OF THE ANGLO-ZULU WAR

determined on June 12 that the visit should no longer be postponed. Cetshwayo was released on his word of honor that he would cooperate with the British authorities.

Cetshwayo boarded the steamship *Arab* on July 12, 1882, bound for England. A crowd cheered as he and three other Zulu chiefs boarded along with the rest of their party. The Anglo-Zulu War had largely been engineered by colonial officials in Africa, as had the immediate fate of Zululand. In the aftermath of the war, however, as the weaknesses of the Wolseley settlement had come to light, the Home Government began taking a stronger hand in the affairs of southern Africa. Nevertheless, it would be up to colonial officials to implement whatever decisions leaders in London made.

CHAPTER 4

The King Returns

LONDONERS HAD HEARD tales of nearly naked Zulu warriors armed with spears and shields who had defeated British forces at Isandhlwana. For this reason, and because most British people at this time viewed Africans as uncivilized, many British people expected the Zulu king to provide a savage spectacle. He had been described by Frere as a "cruel sovereign" who committed "atrocious barbarities" and whose "history is written in characters of blood."

But on the arrival of the *Arab* in England in August 1882, the deposed king cut a smooth and cultivated figure that delighted English society. At ease in his suit and long coat and "crowned" with his headring, Cetshwayo gave off an unmistakable sense of nobility.

TERMS FOR RETURN

During the few weeks of his visit to London, Cetshawyo and the three chiefs who accompanied him met several times with Kimberley, who served as head of the colonial office (the British government office in London that dealt with affairs in British colonies). During the first meeting, Cetshwayo asserted that he had done nothing to provoke war with the British. He also claimed that he had committed no crimes that would justify his removal as king. In his statement, which was summarized in the official record, "Cetshwayo said that he never had any intention of attacking the Queen's dominions [lands under her control], that he had never sent his armies across the border during the war, and that he had been defeated and captured while in his own country." He also answered Kimberley's questions about the reports of his cruelties, denying "any undiscriminate killing such as he had been accused of" and challenging his accusers to point out any specific case of wrongdoing on his part.

While Cetshwayo was awaiting the British government's decision about his fate, Queen Victoria agreed to meet with him personally on August 14, 1882. With Kimberley and the three Zulu chiefs also in attendance, the queen and Cetshwayo had a friendly conversation through an interpreter. She later wrote in her journal that she told Cetshwayo "that I was glad to see him here, and that I recognised in him a great warrior, who had fought against us, but rejoiced we were now friends."

AN 1881 POLITICAL CARTOON FROM *PUNCH* MAGAZINE HIGHLIGHTS BRITISH ATTITUDES TOWARD ZULU PEOPLE, WHO WERE VIEWED BY MANY AS SAVAGES.

Cetshwayo's Arrival in England

ACCORDING TO A BRITISH newspaper report, upon the *Arab*'s arrival in England on August 3, 1882,

> Cetshwayo was dressed in a thick pilot-cloth coat, and wore a cap, under which was a circlet indicating his royal faction [actually the headring worn by all Zulu men of marrying age or older]. He seemed in the best of health and spirits. He has a jet-black face and hair with just a tinge of grey. The King's good temper seemed unbounded. He shook hands heartily with all who bade him welcome to England, laughed and joked with Mr. Shepstone, Mr. Dunn, and his chiefs almost incessantly, and the opinion passed upon him in homely phrase by one of the sailors . . . was that which, after all best seemed to suit him, "a down-right jolly old chap."

On August 15 and 17, Cetshwayo met again with Kimberley, who confirmed that Cetshwayo would be restored to power. However, he would not be restored as an independent leader but as a king who was subordinate to (under the control of) the British Empire. At these meetings, Kimberley outlined terms upon which Cetshwayo would be allowed to return to Zululand. First of all, he would have to give up part of his country, described by the British government as a "strip of territory." That territory would "be reserved for other purposes," although Kimberley assured him that "no more will be reserved than is, in the opinion of the Government, absolutely necessary."

This "strip of territory" was to be set aside as an area where those who did not want to accept Cetshwayo's return could be peacefully resettled. In addition, Cetshwayo would be subject to a British resident and would be bound by fifteen regulations similar to those binding the thirteen appointed chiefs. Cetshwayo would not be allowed to engage in treaties with other governments, choose his successors, or sell any part of his country without British approval. Despite the limitations the terms imposed, Cetshwayo accepted them and prepared for his return to Zululand.

A SMALL STRIP OF LAND

When word of Cetshawayo's resinstatement reached southern Africa, British officials there protested. "I wish to place on record my strong conviction that the return of Cetshwayo to Zululand would be fraught [filled] with considerable danger to Natal, and would give rise to serious trouble and bloodshed in Zululand itself," wrote Wolseley, the high commissioner for southeastern Africa. Other officials, including Bulwer and Osborn, worked to delay the king's return. They used the delays to plan ways to ensure that Cetshwayo would hold even less power and that Zululand would remain divided after his restoration.

Though British officials in southern Africa could not change decisions made in London, they could influence what happened once

The Queen's Impression of Cetshwayo

ALTHOUGH QUEEN VICTORIA was pleased with her meeting with Cetshwayo on August 14, 1882, she was not impressed by his Western clothes. In her journal, she wrote, "Cetewayo [Cetshwayo] is a very fine man, in his native costume, or rather no costume. He is tall, immensely broad, and stout, with a good-humoured countenance [face/expression], and an intelligent face. Unfortunately he appeared in a hideous black frock coat and trousers, but still wearing the ring round his head, denoting [meaning] that he was a married man."

Cetshwayo returned. It was up to them, for example, to set the boundaries of Cetshwayo's new territory. They wanted to create a large buffer area between Zululand and British-ruled Natal, to be governed by Natal. The Natal colonists saw this buffer zone as a place where Zulu people living in Natal could be resettled to open more room in Natal for white settlers. Furthermore, the officials believed Britain was still responsible for providing territories to those appointed chiefs who had supported the Wolseley settlement. So, the kingdom that they defined for Cetshwayo was a much smaller area of land than either Cetshwayo or Kimberley had envisioned.

> *"You efface [make invisible] the Zulu country by your up-and-down slicing [division] of Zululand. What, then, has become of my recent new birth at the hands of our Queen [Victoria]?"*
>
> —Cetshwayo, 1882

First of all, they set aside two strips of land that would not be part of Cetshwayo's domain. One of these would be the buffer on the border between Natal and Zululand. It would be called the Zulu Native Reserve (the Reserve). The other would be a territory in the northeast for Zibhebhu to continue to rule independently.

Zibhebhu was not only a powerful chief but also a favorite of both Osborn and Bulwer, who considered him "a man of considerable force of character, moderate in counsels, strong in action, straightforward in his conduct, courageous, self-reliant." As a counterbalance to Cetshwayo's power, they decided to allow Zibhebhu to rule an independent territory. In the end, Zibhebhu's new territory turned out to be slightly larger than what he had received in the Wolseley settlement.

None of the other appointed chiefs were to remain independent, however. Dunn and another of the appointed chiefs, Hlubi, would remain on their lands, which became part of the Zulu Native Reserve. However, they would be reduced to the status of lower chiefs under the new British resident commissioner of the Reserve, John Shepstone (brother of Theophilus). In addition to providing an

area where these two chiefs could remain outside of Cetshwayo's territory, Bulwer also claimed that the Reserve would provide refuge to "great numbers of the Zulu people [who] have no wish to return under [Cetshwayo's] rule."

CETSHWAYO RETURNS TO ZULULAND

While officials in Zululand were slicing away at the portion of Zululand that Cetshwayo would be allowed to rule, Cetshwayo was sent again to Oude Molen. There, a smallpox quarantine was used as a reason to keep him away from Zululand from September through December 1883.

In December Cetshwayo was asked to sign a document agreeing to additional demands made by Bulwer, including the changes

An 1883 wood engraving depicts Cetshwayo at Oude Molen awaiting his reinstatement as Zulu king.

that would reduce his kingdom by more than one-third of its land. Fearing that if he did not sign, he would not be allowed to return, Cetshwayo signed, but under protest.

Finally, on January 10, 1883, Cetshwayo returned to his former kingdom. But even as he was re-instated, local colonial officials did much to discredit his authority. When Cetshwayo arrived at Port Durnford in the Zulu Native Reserve, he was met by only a small welcoming party that included Theophilus Shepstone, some soldiers and policemen, and a few Zulu people. More Zulu well-wishers might have come to greet their king had the exact date of his return not been purposely kept vague. In fact, many Zulu people, including Mnyamana, did not believe Cetshwayo was being returned to Zululand until they saw him with their own eyes.

However, as soon as it became known that Cetshwayo was actually in Zululand, the Zulu people began gathering to welcome him. "And all that day as we went, we kept meeting streams of people going to the King, having now heard for certain that it was he himself," reported one of the Zulu men who accompanied the party.

Local British officials continued their efforts to lessen Cetshwayo's authority. The honor guard (military escort for a ceremonial occasion) that the officials arranged to accompany Cetshwayo and Shepstone to the reinstallation ceremony consisted of about 430 white soldiers and about 60 black African attendants. This huge escort party left the impression that the king was still a prisoner. This military force also caused much fear among the Zulu onlookers, and Shepstone noticed "a very serious distrust of, and disbelief in our professed [stated] intentions."

The honor guard also served another purpose. Osborn had told Theophilus Shepstone that Cetshwayo had ordered the uSuthu to come armed to the reinstallation ceremony. For this reason, Shepstone feared for his own safety and insisted on the presence of the honor guard. Shepstone even demanded of Cetshwayo "that the Zulus, and especially the young men, should not approach the camp [where Shepstone and Cetshwayo would stay until the ceremony],

An Agreement Signed under Protest

"MR. J. MULLINS [a trader who did business in Zululand] said, 'I asked the King how came he to agree to conditions [for his return as king] such as we had heard of? He said, "It was not that I agreed to them. I had no choice given me. I was told that the country [Zululand] was to be cut off from the Umhlatuze, and that to the north also a large piece was to be cut off for Zibebu [Zibhebhu]; and that if I did not sign, I should never return, but remain always at the Cape [under house arrest]. So I signed under protest, knowing that the land belongs to my people, and that I had no right to sign it away without their consent, and trusting that, as the English Government have listened to my prayer once, they will do so again and set this thing right, and restore us to our country."'"

—Cetshwayo, quoted in the *Cape Times,* December 30, 1882

or be present at the ceremony of installation, armed, and that I should prefer that the young men be kept away altogether."

THE REINSTALLATION OF CETSHWAYO

On January 17, 1883, about six thousand Zulu supporters of Cetshwayo had gathered at Emtonjaneni (in what is now Mtonjaneni, KwaZulu-Natal, South Africa), where the reinstallation ceremony was to take place. "They went to the King, and then to Somtseu (Sir T. Shepstone), and then back to the King, where all the crowds of Zulus had formed a circle, and were singing the songs of Tshaka [Shaka, first Zulu king]. The King sat and talked with mothers and wives, telling them about his journey, and now and then calling out some one to speak with him," recalled a witness.

The reinstallation ceremony took place on January 29, 1883, when a last group of uSuthu from the north finally arrived. Dinuzulu, Cetshwayo's son, was present. A newspaper report on the ceremony described Dinuzulu as "the image of his father, and so fat that, although only 14 years of age, he must weigh at least that number of stone [196 pounds]. . . . He was evidently fully alive to his position, as he trod [walked] the earth as if he owned it. In receiving the congratulations of the numerous Indunas he maintained a *sang-froid* [composure] worthy of his birth."

The Zulu audience sat in a semicircle in front of Shepstone, while Cetshwayo sat to his right and a British military officer to his left. Then Shepstone publicly read out the conditions of Cetshwayo's reinstatement, further illustrating Cetshwayo's lack of true power. The pronouncement upset the uSuthu, because this was the first official announcement of the new division of Zululand. However, Cetshwayo accepted his position. He even asked Shepstone to issue

the command for the Zulu men to build the king a kraal rather than commanding them himself to do so. That way, it could not be said that he had assembled any regiments.

After Shepstone read out the conditions, the chiefs addressed him. Shepstone had believed that the Zulu masses would oppose the restoration of "a dreaded ruler upon unwilling people." In fact, some Zulu audience members did express disappointment but not over Cetshwayo's reinstatement. Their disappointment was based on the terms of his return to power. They complained that the Zulu Native Reserve was too large. More of the territory should have been returned to Cetshwayo, they believed. They also spoke out against Zibhebhu, whom they accused "of every kind of violence and atrocity, and of

The Only King in Zululand

"WHILE CETSHWAYO IS subject to the English Government in many things, and rules his country only in conjunction with the British Resident attached to him, Zibebu [Zibhebhu] is free of any such restraint, and therefore practically enjoys more power in Zululand, and holds a higher position, than Cetshwayo himself. It would not be unfair to compare Cetshwayo to a chief in Zululand . . . and at the same time it can be said without fear of contradiction that Zibebu is now the only King in Zululand."

—*Times of Natal,* February 17, 1883

being a persistent disturber of the peace of the country." Mayepu, an uSuthu, made more specific accusations: "Sir, can we say that you *are* restoring him? No, you are killing him! There are daughters of mine belonging to the royal household who have been taken by Zibebu [Zibhebhu]. All have perished, girls, cattle, and land! Do you think that we brought forth children for a dog like that? I would rather cut my throat before you here." Even Zibhebhu's brothers, from whom Zibhebhu had seized cattle because they had been kept in uSuthu kraals during the deputations, protested the situation.

THE STAGE FOR CIVIL WAR

Under the terms of Cetshwayo's restoration in 1883, several obstacles hindered his ability to rule effectively. First was the problem of the Zulu Native Reserve, land Cetshwayo had lost and that he referred to as "the best pieces of the country" and where "the original Zulus live." This territory was originally the Zulu heartland, the area from which the Zulu nation had arisen under Shaka. It still included the lands of many of the most faithful uSuthu, including Cetshwayo's half brother Dabulamanzi, who had called so loudly for Cetshwayo's return. The Zulu Native Reserve was also home to Dunn, now Cetshwayo's enemy. Furthermore, British colonial leaders in Natal encouraged people who lived in Cetshwayo's existing territories to move to the Reserve if they disagreed with the policies of the king. The Reserve thus was home to some of Cetshwayo's bitterest enemies as well as his strongest supporters. As a result, it became a hotbed of discontent.

In addition, the British had seized all of Cetshwayo's royal cattle, the source of wealth and power in Zulu society, and the herds of his relatives had grown smaller on account of raids by Zibhebhu and Hamu. Some of Cetshwayo's supporters donated cattle to him. Yet this stripped Cetshwayo of even more dignity. since Zulu culture at that time called for the king to reward his people with cattle, not the reverse.

Worst of all, though, was the fact that Zibhebhu remained independent and ruled over a territory that encompassed the land of many of Cetshwayo's supporters. While Cetshwayo's people were engaged in building the royal kraal and were not permitted to arm, the warriors of Zibhebhu's Mandlakazi group were drilling for modern combat. Some units even practiced firing rifles from horseback. Cetshwayo had been restored as Zulu king in name. But with no real power, no armies, and hemmed in between enemies in the Reserve and in Zibhebhu's territory, it became clear that he would not remain king for long.

CHAPTER 5

A New Republic Rises

COWED INTO OBEDIENCE, Cetshwayo stuck to the terms of his reinstatement. He was prohibited from arming or organizing an army, and so he did not create one. Zibhebhu, on the other hand, paid little attention to Wolseley's laws. He built a strong fighting force and trained his men in the use of arms and horses. He did this with help from some white mercenaries (soldiers who fight for payment). As the *Times of Natal* reported on June 24, 1882, Zibhebhu had the "means to obtain firearms; and many of his followers already not only possess firearms, but know how to use them."

In March 1883, Zibhebhu sent men to claim the uSuthu kraals that had become part of his territory. Most of the uSuthu were still away with Cetshwayo, and although the few who remained fought back, they were easily overpowered. Cetshwayo urged restraint, but between four thousand and six thousand uSuthu gathered and marched northward, intending to recapture the kraals. They were no match for Zibhebhu's better-armed and better-trained forces. When the two sides met on March 30, 1883, the uSuthu were easily dispersed.

Zibhebhu, allied now with Hamu, followed up the rout of the uSuthu by threatening Cetshwayo. Cetshwayo appealed to colonial authorities in Natal for assistance, since he had no army of his own. They refused to assist because they considered the uSuthu to have started the fight by attempting to retake the uSuthu kraals.

As soon as he discovered that the British would not support Cetshwayo, Zibhebhu sent his armed horsemen to Ulundi. A witness reported afterward:

> The sun was just up, and large parties of the men were away, some having gone to their wood-cutting, some to the river to wash,

In January 1883, Cetshwayo, center, seated, and the remains of his family returned under British escort to his much diminished realm. This image is from an illustration by Frank Dadd in *The Illustrated London News* (1883).

others to fetch water, some were escorting home the parties of girls who had come bringing food to the royal kraal, while those who remained were not kept in any particular order; while the kraal was full of women too who were preparing the thatch of the huts.

Zibhebhu and his men descended upon this scene on July 21, 1883, "rushing unprovoked on the [royal] Ondini Kraal and massacring all and sundry," reported the Natal *Adviser*. Cetshwayo himself escaped with two assegai (iron-tipped spear) wounds and fled to the Nkandhla forest. Dinuzulu also escaped and later joined his father at his hideout near the Mome Gorge, a gorge formed by the Mome stream that flowed through the Nkandhla forest. On this day, many of the most powerful chiefs in Zululand were killed or forced to flee.

On October 15, 1883, Cetshwayo went to Eshowe to seek help from Osborn. Osborn had been named resident commissioner of the Zulu Native Reserve after Cetshwayo's return. Osborn offered no help. Instead, he disbanded Cetshwayo's followers. In despair over the fate of his people and unable to launch a counterattack back into his own territory, Cetshwayo remained in exile in Eshowe.

DEATH OF CETSHWAYO

Almost four months later, after an afternoon meal on February 8, 1884, Cetshwayo suffered from a convulsion and died suddenly at the age of around 51. Cetshwayo's brothers Dabulamanzi and Ndabuko, his induna Mnyamana, and other notable uSuthu were with him at Eshowe when he died. Dabulamanzi's son later related Cetshwayo's dying words: "Dabulamanzi, take care of this child of mine, Dinuzulu, for me. Dinuzulu is my only son. Bring him up properly. I leave him with you, you who are nearest in my house."

A British military doctor performed an examination of Cetshwayo's body immediately. The official doctor's report listed the cause of death as heart disease, which may have been brought on by a diet consisting largely of beef and a long imprisonment during which Cetshwayo had exercised little. The uSuthu believed otherwise. They believed Cetshwayo had been poisoned, and they believed agents of Zibhebhu were to blame. Those who believed in the poisoning claimed that uSuthu witnesses had seen him healthy all morning, so his death seemed to have been caused by something he ate.

The uSuthu wished to bury their leader at the Zulu royal burial ground in the sacred eMakhosini Valley or at Chief Lohunu's kraal in the Nkandhla forest. Osborn refused permission to bury him at either location, suggesting instead that they bury him at Eshowe. After two months, Cetshwayo still had not been buried. Finally, on April 8, Cetshwayo's widows entered Osborn's headquarters and demanded Cetshwayo's burial. Osborn compromised, permitting the burial to proceed at one of Dabulamanzi's kraals near Eshowe.

However, due to the rough condition of the region's mountain roads, the ox-drawn wagon carrying Cetshwayo's body could not reach the approved site. The uSuthu feared they would never receive what they considered fair treatment from colonial officials, and Osborn's attitude seemed an example of the impossibility of their situation. So Cetshwayo's brothers decided to go to the burial site at Lohunu's kraal and begin the burial ceremonies on April 10, 1884. The funeral could not be conducted entirely in peace. A group of Zulu Native Reserve police interrupted to demand that Ndabuko immediately pay his hut tax (a tax on each of the huts a Zulu man owned).

When Osborn heard that the funeral was being held at Lohunu's kraal instead of at Dabulamanzi's kraal, he began to arm forces to oppose what he considered an act of rebellion. He sent two messengers to Mnyamana, but some of the uSuthu stabbed the messengers with assegais. This attack confirmed to Osborn his idea that the uSuthu were rebelling. In response, Osborn ordered the confiscation of the cattle of all the people who crossed the border into Zululand to join the uSuthu. Furthermore, he refused to accept the uSuthu claim that Cetshwayo's son Dinuzulu was the rightful heir to the kingship of Zululand.

TROUBLE IN ZULULAND AND THE RESERVE

Since the British authorities of Natal would not mediate between the uSuthu and Zibhebhu, the uSuthu leaders felt the need to ally with another power to counterbalance Zibhebhu and his white soldiers. For this reason, some of the uSuthu leaders suggested engaging in talks with Boers from the Transvaal. But the older uSuthu leaders knew from experience that Boers were likely to claim Zulu lands in return for any favors they did for the uSuthu. Mnyamana in particular hesitated to ask Boers for help. He knew that Zululand had lost much of its territory to Boers and that even more would have been lost if the British had not intervened.

"Do not dare to treat [make deals] with the Boers, for if you once get them into the country you will never get rid of them."

—Cetshwayo, 1884

While the older uSuthu debated, some of the younger men took matters into their own hands. They explained their situation to some Boers who lived on the border of the South African Republic. These

THE AFTERMATH OF THE ANGLO-ZULU WAR

Complex Alliances

MILITARY ALLEGIANCES BETWEEN various African groups and British and Boer settlers were rarely clear-cut, with black Africans on one side and white colonists on the other. From the time of Shaka, white groups had fought with the Zulu armies against their African enemies. And during British or Boer attacks on African groups or on each other, they often enlisted the assistance of other local groups.

Sometimes these alliances became long-term. Hlubi, chief of the Basuto group, was a prominent example of an African chief who staunchly supported the British. Hlubi's men fought for the British on numerous occasions. In return, the Wolseley settlement named Hlubi one of the thirteen appointed chiefs in Zululand, in spite of the fact that he and his people did not even come from Zululand.

Boers promised to help the uSuthu to end the troubles in Zululand. Once they took action, it was too late for Mnyamana's objections to have any effect.

The assistance that the Boers raised did not take the form of official action by the South African Republic. Instead, on May 1, 1884, a group of about eight hundred armed fortune seekers, mostly Boers from the Transvaal, entered Zululand and established a military camp near Hlobane Mountain. They sent messengers to Zibhebhu and Hamu, saying they had come to establish peace in Zululand under Dinuzulu. They demanded that Zibhebhu's and Hamu's men disarm and withdraw to their territories.

Meanwhile, the situation in the Zulu Native Reserve continued to deteriorate. Cattle seizures ordered by Osborn continued, and some uSuthu chiefs responded with counterraids, which led to more skirmishes between British troops and the uSuthu. A larger clash occurred on May 10 when an army of more than two thousand uSuthu approached two British government columns of African troops commanded by British officers. The uSuthu attacked, but their lack of training showed. When they fired their guns, most fired too high. The government troops, on the other hand, fired in a steady and organized fashion. The clash resulted in heavy losses for the uSuthu and only one government soldier killed and one wounded.

The government forces withdrew to Eshowe. At the same time, Osborn requested British troops to support his men in the Reserve and Zibhebhu's men in Zululand. Bulwer, the governor of Natal, relayed this request to Britain's secretary of colonial affairs in London. Bulwer had recently called for Britain to annex Zululand. He claimed that the uSuthu were on the verge of invading Zululand. The secretary of colonial affairs replied by telegram that Zululand would not be annexed, nor would it be protected by Britain. However, he wanted local colonial officials to maintain peace within the Reserve.

THE CORONATION OF DINUZULU

After Cetshwayo's death, his brothers decided that Zululand needed a king to lead the movement to recapture Cetshwayo's territory. So on May 20, 1884, they prepared the sixteen-year-old prince Dinuzulu to succeed his father as Zulu king. At the Zulu coronation ceremony, Mnyamana was conspicuously absent. His absence was probably in protest of the uSuthu's continued dealings with Boers. Dinuzulu and the other princes proceeded without him. The next day, following in his grandfather Mpande's footsteps, Dinuzulu allowed a representative of the Boer group to crown him. In a ceremony designed to remind observers of Mpande's coronation, when Mpande lost half his lands to Boers, the Boer group declared Dinuzulu to be Cetshwayo's heir and the king of Zululand.

Following his coronation, Dinuzulu signed a treaty with these Boers. In the treaty, the Boers promised military assistance against the "rebels" in his territory. In return, Dinuzulu promised he would turn over to them a piece of land of unspecified size from northwestern Zululand.

THE BATTLE OF TSHANENI

Zibhebhu refused to give cattle, land, or allegiance to Dinuzulu and refused to recognize him as king. In response, one hundred men from the Boer camp at Hlobane accompanied about ten thousand uSuthu warriors as they marched on Zibhebhu's Mandlakazi forces.

The combined uSuthu and Boer force encountered Zibhebhu's people on June 5, 1884. Zibhebhu had arranged an ambush at a gorge where the Mkusi River passes through the Lebombo Mountains near Mount Tshaneni. His army of around three thousand soldiers was hidden on the riverbank. The women and cattle were hidden to the north of the river. The uSuthu, followed by the Boers, approached unaware, but cautiously, and they discovered their enemies before the Mandlakazi could take advantage of their trap. However, the Mandlakazi were very familiar with the territory and had undergone intense training, so they were able at first to beat back the uSuthu.

Cetshwayo's Other Son

NOT EVERYONE ACCEPTED Dinuzulu as Cetshwayo's heir. When Cetshwayo died in 1884, his principal wife was pregnant. Many people believed that her son, Manzolwandle (*water of the ocean,*" named after Cetshwayo's trip to England), should become king. One reason for this was that Cetshwayo and Dinuzulu's mother were not married when Dinuzulu was born. However, the principal uSuthu chiefs supported Dinuzulu and overrode any objections to make him king.

Many uSuthu were slain, and the Mandlakazi pressed their advantage. When the Boers began shooting, the Mandlakazi fled toward the river. The Boers withdrew after the Mandlakazi scattered, but the uSuthu kept up the attack. Before the Mandlakazi warriors could cross the river, where their women and children were hiding, one group of warriors on the uSuthu side moved in on the women, children, and cattle. They captured as many as they could. Zibhebhu and his white advisers had watched the battle from a ridge. They escaped and hid in nearby mountain caves. Altogether, the battle of Tshaneni lasted about an hour, but after it was over, the uSuthu continued to slay fleeing Mandlakazi and to capture around sixty thousand cattle.

THE NEW REPUBLIC

In the aftermath of the decisive uSuthu win, the Boer group decided they had fulfilled the terms of the treaty and requested the land the uSuthu had promised them. The Boers felt that Britain could no longer claim responsibility for Zululand and that they—a foreign power—were legally justified in dealing directly with the Zulu leaders. Although Cetshwayo's agreement with the British required that Zulu leaders not give territory to other powers, Zibhebhu had, in effect, conquered the country. Since the British government had not defended Zululand from Zibhebhu, as much as it belonged to any power it belonged to Zibhebhu. Since the uSuthu, backed by Boers, had defeated Zibhebhu, they had the right to make policy in the country, including the right to give away territory. In the Boer group's view Zululand had been in a state of anarchy (absence of government) for almost five years and without British intervention to improve the situation. In fact, the British government had refused to intervene during this entire time. Therefore, the Boer group believed, agreements between the British government and Cetshwayo in 1882 did not apply to the uSuthu leaders in 1884.

By June 1884, the Boer camp in Zululand consisted of more than eight hundred armed men, all of whom demanded farms in Zululand. Negotiations for the land were stalled by the uSuthu, especially Mnyamana, who argued that the Mandlakazi had been defeated in

Murder of Dabulamanzi

THE USUTHU LEADER Dabulamanzi, Cetshwayo's half brother whom Cetshwayo chose to care for his son Dinuzulu after his death, was killed in the aftermath of the establishment of the New Republic in 1884. Some New Republic settlers accused Dabulamanzi and his son of stealing cattle. When they denied this charge, the men got into a heated argument, and one of the settlers shot Dabulamanzi.

THIS HAND-COLORED LANTERN SLIDE FROM THE 1800S DEPICTS CETSHWAYO'S HALF BROTHER DABULAMANZI, CENTER.

only a single battle and that any talk of awarding land to the Boer group should wait until Zululand was at peace. Furthermore, Mnyamana insisted, if any farms were to be awarded to Boers, they would be awarded only to the one hundred men who had participated in the battle against the Mandlakazi. The Boer group then tried a new tactic. Rather than deal with Mnyamana and with Cetshwayo's brothers, they began to deal directly with young Dinuzulu. Seeing the Boers as a means to the restoration of his royal glory, and helpless before the potential threat posed by an armed camp of more than eight hundred Boers, Dinuzulu yielded.

On August 16, 1884, Dinuzulu signed a treaty with the Boer group, granting them 1,355,000 morgen of land. A morgen was an old Dutch unit of area equal to slightly more than 2 acres (1 ha). In total, the Boers' claim, then, was approximately 2,720,000 acres (1,100,745 ha). This land was to be the beginnings of a new country called the New Republic. It would be bordered by the Zulu Native Reserve and the South African Republic on the south and the west. No eastern boundary was defined, however. What remained of Zululand was also to be supervised by the New Republic.

Dinuzulu did not fully understand how much land he had signed away to the Boer group, and the uSuthu leaders thought that it was a smaller area than it turned out to be. The Boers believed that amount of land would be sufficient for exactly eight hundred large Boer farms. Even the Boers did not actually realize what a large percentage of Zululand their new home would take up. In fact, it was more than one-third of what remained of the country.

BRITAIN'S INTEREST IN ZULULAND

Boers began work on their new farms almost immediately, starting with a land survey. Once that survey was completed in May 1885, Boers set

An engraving from 1890 depicts a typical Boer farm in Zululand and the Transvaal.

out for their new farms. In some cases, the Boers encountered Zulu families living on their land. The Boers either drove them away or told them they could stay and work as laborers for the farm's new owner.

Conflict grew when Dinuzulu, finally understanding the impact of the treaty, reversed his position and announced that the Boers had no right to land in Zululand. Zulu warriors raided the new Boer farms, and Boers responded by burning Zulu kraals, seizing their livestock, and chasing them off with guns. Some of the Zulu families who had been displaced by Boers went into hiding in nearby caves; others moved onto land that Boers had not yet claimed. Thrown off of their lands and unable to grow food, the people of Zululand began to suffer from a growing food shortage. Poverty further increased in Zululand due to a black market (illegal) trade in food and guns from Natal. The traders were able to charge very high prices, and many people in Zululand had to spend their remaining wealth for food or guns to defend themselves.

THE NEW COLONIAL SECRETARY, LORD GRANVILLE, TOOK GREATER INTEREST IN AFFAIRS IN ZULULAND THAN HIS PREDECESSOR HAD.

All the while, the British government looked on but took no meaningful action. As the Boer surveyors continued making official measurements of land acquired in Zululand ever farther east, the British had placed flags and signs along Zululand's St. Lucia Bay. These signs declared the area British territory. Nevertheless, Britain did nothing when the surveyors ignored the signs, surveyed the land for farms, and advertised their sale in newspapers in the British colony of Natal. On October 26, 1885, the New Republic went a step further, expanding its own boundaries so that it covered more than 80 percent of Zululand. The British government protested but took no substantive action.

The loss of Zulu land had grown so extreme that Mnyamana and the uSuthu delivered yet another plea to Osborn for British assistance. Osborn forwarded this plea, along with his own request for British intervention in Zululand, to Sir Charles Mitchell. Mitchell had replaced Bulwer as acting governor of Natal and sent the request to London.

With changes in government at home, Great Britain responded to the plea. These changes included a new colonial secretary, Lord Granville, who had taken office and was interested in the affairs of Zululand. On March 11, 1886, he empowered Lord Arthur Havelock, the new governor of Natal, to negotiate with the New Republic. Britain was willing to accept occupation by the New Republic of a certain amount of the territory they had claimed in Zululand but asserted that the New Republic's deal with Dinuzulu was invalid. In Havelock's negotiations with the New Republic, he stated that Zulu leaders were not permitted to negotiate with foreign powers (such as the Boer group) or give away land without British authorization. Havelock made it clear that Britain had not authorized the deals the uSuthu had made with the Boer group. Havelock's negotiations, however, were fruitless for several months.

TREATY BETWEEN GREAT BRITAIN AND THE NEW REPUBLIC

In the aftermath of the New Republic's laying claim to most of Zululand, British interest in affairs in Zululand had increased. Havelock persisted and eventually managed to arrange a new set of negotiations between Great Britain and the New Republic. British officials now stepped in, but not as allies coming to assist independent Zulu leaders. The negotiations that would determine control of lands in Zululand were between Great Britain and the New Republic. Zulu leaders could not even involve their representatives in the negotiations.

This new set of negotiations was held from October 18 to October 22, 1886. Havelock represented the British government, and Acting President Lucas Meyer and others represented the New Republic. This time, seeing that Britain had a serious interest in Zululand affairs, the New Republic agreed to a treaty. The treaty reduced the territory of the New Republic somewhat. It allowed more of the Boers who had already settled areas outside the new boundaries to remain where they were, but if they did, their farms would be in

Zululand, not the New Republic. And the New Republic had to give up its claim of sovereignty over Zululand. In return, Britain would recognize the New Republic as an independent nation.

In November 1886, Cetshwayo's brother Shingana met with Governor Havelock to protest the absence of Zulu representatives during the October negotiations with the New Republic. He claimed that only the original one hundred Boers who assisted at Mount Tshaneni should have any right to territory. Havelock replied that there was nothing the uSuthu could do about it. It was, after all, uSuthu leaders who had signed the country over to the Boer group in the first place. The uSuthu then asked for the return of the Emakosini Valley, the sacred place where their kings had been buried. This valley had been converted into a number of Boer farms. The British officials were content with Havelock's deal with the New Republic, though, and the sacred valley would remain in white hands for more than a century to come.

CHAPTER 6

Britain Asserts Control

WITH THE NEGOTIATIONS between Great Britain and the New Republic, the expansion of the New Republic had been halted. Yet Zululand remained weak and divided. This worried British officials in Natal. They knew that the New Republic might make another try to expand their territory. Or another foreign power might attempt a takeover. (European nations were very interested in taking control of African nations at this time in history. They hoped for wealth in extracting the continent's many resources.) Furthermore, with no powerful government in Zululand, civil war could break out at any moment. With so many Zulu people living in Natal, this also posed a threat to Natal's stability.

The Natal Legislative Council proposed to deal with these problems by annexing Zululand. The proposed annexation would take in the Zulu Native Reserve and what remained of Zululand outside of the New Republic. That way, Zululand would become a part of

Natal. It would be British territory, protected by the British military from outside invaders. Inside Zululand, Natalian colonial police forces would keep order and enforce the laws of Natal. Many in Natal also hoped that Zululand could then be opened to white colonists.

However, the colonial secretary in London did not grant Natal's annexation request. Local African people who lived under chiefs in Natal were governed by different laws than those who lived in Zululand. Annexation by Natal would place residents of Zululand under the same laws, known as the Native Law code. This included the hut tax. The colonial secretary did not consider Natal's Native Laws appropriate to Zululand. Nor did he believe that Natal could cover the cost of ruling Zululand. He and other officials in London, however, did recognize the security threat that the current state of

THE NATIVE LAW CODE INCLUDED A HUT TAX. A NINETEENTH-CENTURY WOODCUT SHOWS ZULU MEN LINING UP TO PAY THEIR HUT TAXES.

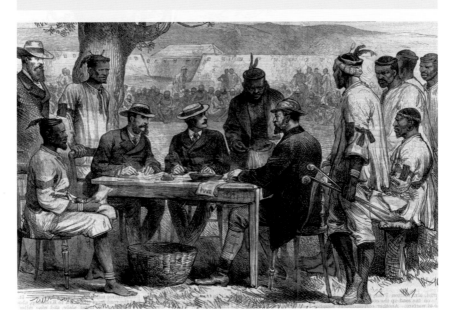

THE AFTERMATH OF THE ANGLO-ZULU WAR

Zululand represented to Natal. They had also heard that Boers who had been allowed to keep farms in Zululand had been mistreating the Zulu people there. They agreed that something had to be done to strengthen the rule of law in Zululand.

Osborn, in the Reserve, believed that the instability of Zululand demanded immediate attention. Since Zululand could not be annexed by Natal, on February 5, 1887, Osborn sent messengers to Zululand to announce that Zululand was to become a protectorate of Britain. This meant it would be protected and ruled by the British Empire, even if it would not be directly governed by the government of Natal. The British government approved extension of protectorate status, although approval came after Osborn had already made his announcement.

Following this approval, the British government also agreed to formally annex Zululand into the British Empire. Thus Zululand became part of the British Empire in May 1887, although Zululand was to remain a separate entity from the Natal colony. The annexation and protectorate status applied only to the portion of Zululand that remained outside of the New Republic and the Reserve. It did not affect Britain's October 1886 border agreement with the New Republic.

Under the new arrangement, Zululand was to be divided into eleven districts, with each district governed by a local resident magistrate appointed by the British government. The chiefs who lived in the area would remain where they were and would rule under their local resident magistrate. Their rule would be subject to the magistrates' approval.

They could not, for example, apply a death sentence without a trial before the magistrate, even if Zulu law called for immediate execution. While the Natal colony would not rule Zululand, the Natal Native Law code and the hut tax were extended over Zululand in spite of the earlier objections by the colonial secretary.

The proclamation of Zululand's new protectorate status was made at Eshowe before a gathering of nine thousand to fifteen thousand Zulu people, including several powerful chiefs. Osborn became the resident commissioner and chief magistrate of Zululand.

"THE HOUSE OF SHAKA IS A THING OF THE PAST"

In the aftermath of the proclamation, most of the Zulu chiefs accepted Zululand's new status as a British protectorate. But Dinuzulu and some of the uSuthu leaders objected to several terms that were part of the change. They most objected to the fact that many of the Zulu people still remained in the New Republic under the current border agreements. Furthermore, they did not favor the implementation of Natal Native Law and the hut tax. Dinuzulu almost immediately began to clash with Dick Addison, the resident magistrate appointed to the Ndwandwe district where he lived. Dinuzulu refused to pay the fines he had been told to pay for enforcing Zulu laws without British approval. He refused to accept the stipend (payment) offered to him by the British to rule under their authority. And he crossed the border to the New Republic to negotiate with Boers there without first obtaining permission from British authorities. He also maintained regiments armed with rifles. More than once, these regiments confronted police who came to enforce the British requirements.

British officials, frustrated by Dinuzulu's refusal to cooperate, repeatedly summoned Dinuzulu and the chiefs who supported him to appear before them. Not until November 1887 did Dinuzulu finally meet with Havelock, Natal's governor. At that November 14 meeting, Havelock criticized Dinuzulu before several other uSuthu princes and chiefs. He announced: "Dinuzulu must know that the rule of the House of Shaka is a thing of the past. It is dead. It is like water spilt on the ground. The Queen now rules in Zululand and no one else." The governor confirmed that Dinuzulu was still responsible for paying the fines and that Dinuzulu, as a chief (not a king), must obey the magistrate like any other chief.

DINUZULU, SHOWN HERE IN 1887 IN THE NEW REPUBLIC, REFUSED TO PAY FINES LEVIED AGAINST HIM FOR ENFORCING ZULU LAWS WITHOUT BRITISH APPROVAL.

Even worse news for Dinuzulu and the uSuthu followed. After the Battle of Tshaneni, Zibhebhu had taken several thousand of his Mandlakazi to live in the Reserve under Osborn's jurisdiction (legal authority). As long as the Mandlakazi remained there, hostilities between the Mandlakazi and uSuthu were mostly under control. However, on November 15, 1887, Dinuzulu and the chiefs learned that Zibhebhu would be allowed to return to his former territory. Much of this territory was also in the Ndwandwe district, where Dinuzulu lived. Although Zibhebhu would return not as an independent chief but as a chief subject to the resident magistrate, the uSuthu considered many of the lands he claimed to be uSuthu lands.

The Final Battle between Dinuzulu and Zibhebhu

Dinuzulu assembled a force of five hundred armed men to protest Zibhebhu's return. He led these men to Resident Magistrate Dick Addison's Ndwandwe district headquarters at Ivuna on December 8, 1887, to tell Addison in person how offended he was that Zibhebhu was allowed to return. A few weeks later, Zibhebhu made an even greater show of force, bringing more than a thousand of his armed men to Ivuna to demand the removal of the uSuthu from his territory. Dinuzulu further escalated the situation by increasing his armed force to more than fifteen hundred men.

Assisted by a military force, Addison attempted to separate the uSuthu from the Mandlakazi. He insisted that the uSuthu move off of land that he considered Zibhebhu's and that the Mandlakazi move off of uSuthu lands.

Not content with Addison's response to Zibhebhu, Dinuzulu began to prepare for war. He appealed for assistance from the New Republic and then from the Swazi kingdom, a powerful independent nation to the north. Neither wanted to anger the British, however, and they refused Dinuzulu's appeal.

uSuthu on Zibhebhu's Land

WHEN FLEEING FROM the Boers of the New Republic in 1885–1886, many uSuthu had built kraals in Zibhebhu's former territories. So when Zibhebhu and his Mandlakazi arrived back in northeastern Zululand from the former Zulu Native Reserve in December 1887, they found uSuthu kraals built and uSuthu crops planted on the lands Zibhebhu had occupied.

Despite these setbacks, Dinuzulu pushed ahead with his plans for war. With Ndabuko's help, he established his base at Ceza Mountain, about 23 miles (37 km) to the southwest of Ivuna. For food supplies, his men raided nearby cattle ranches.

Dinuzulu's rebellion at first met with a few successes. On June 2, 1888, a group of Zululand police and British imperial soldiers approached Dinuzulu's camp at Ceza Mountain to arrest Dinuzulu and Ndabuko for cattle theft. Dinuzulu's men were stationed on a plateau high up on the mountain. Sixty-six policemen and 140 dragoons (soldiers trained to fight on foot but who ride horses for transportation and some fighting), backed by 400 of Mnyamana's warriors who had refused to join Dinuzulu against the British, moved in. When the police fired, Dinuzulu's men surrounded the government forces and even more warriors jumped up out of the brush and joined the attack. Government forces lost only five men—two killed and three wounded—but they retreated when their ammunition began to run low.

Encouraged by the victory at Ceza Mountain, Dinuzulu marched his army south toward the Nongoma magistracy headquarters. There Zibhebhu had been holding his men in reserve, and Mandlakazi warriors had recently killed several uSuthu supporters. On June 23, as Dinuzulu's men neared Ivuna, Osborn feared an attack on the headquarters. So he gathered around fifty policemen to take up a defensive position in a fort there. About 1,000 yards (914 m) away from the fort, Zibhebhu

> **FAST FACT**
>
> UNLIKE HIS FATHER, DINUZULU PREFERRED, LIKE THE GREAT SHAKA, TO PARTICIPATE IN WAR ALONG WITH HIS WARRIORS. IN THE JUNE 23, 1888, BATTLE AGAINST ZIBHEBHU AT IVUNA, HE IS SAID TO HAVE KILLED FIVE OF THE MANDLAKAZI WARRIORS HIMSELF.

and his force of approximately 750 men prepared for battle. At first, it appeared that Dinuzulu intended to attack both positions. One thousand of his men headed toward the fort while the other three thousand held back. However, rather than attacking the fort, Dinuzulu's advance force cut off Zibhebhu's men to prevent them from reaching the safety of the fort. Dinuzulu's other three thousand warriors attacked the Mandlakazi. During the ensuing battle, about 200 of Zibhebhu's men were killed and 60 wounded. The rest, including Zibhebhu, fled. Zibhebhu made his way back to the fortress the next day, and he reluctantly joined the police as they retreated and abandoned the fort. Altogether, Dinuzulu had lost about forty men, while his army captured a considerable number of cattle, women, and children.

Dinuzulu's Surrender and Exile

Before Zululand had become British territory in May 1887, British forces had mostly stayed out of internal Zulu conflicts. But with Zululand as a British protectorate, Dinuzulu was seen as a rebel. Once British forces got involved, Dinuzulu's cause was lost. On July 2, 1888, British forces of more than two thousand men surrounded a camp led by Dinuzulu's uncle Shingana. Initially, Shingana's much smaller force held out against government forces. Eventually, though, the soldiers' superior numbers and weapons forced the Zulu fighters to retreat. Shingana escaped to the New Republic.

Next, government troops took up positions around Zululand. Dinuzulu and Ndabuko realized that they would not be able to go on fighting. Therefore, along with about sixteen hundred of their followers, they crossed into the South African Republic. Recognizing that their fight was lost, both leaders secretly made their way back into British territory to peacefully face arrest and trial. Ndabuko surrendered at

DINUZULU, CENTER, VISITS WITH A GROUP OF WHITE MISSIONARY SUPPORTERS DURING HIS 1889 TRIAL ON A CHARGE OF HIGH TREASON.

a military camp near Ivuna on September 16. Dinuzulu was peacefully arrested at the home of a European friend in Natal on November 12.

From February to April 1889, Shingana, Ndabuko, and Dinuzulu were tried for various crimes, including "public violence" for taking up arms against Zibhebhu without permission. The charge on which all of them were convicted was high treason. Ndabuko was sentenced to fifteen years in prison, Shingana to twelve, and Dinuzulu to ten.

Fearing a backlash of violence from the men's followers, British authorities sent them into exile on the faraway island of St. Helena in the South Atlantic Ocean. On St. Helena, Dinuzulu and his uncles lived in a large house about 4 miles (6 km) from the island's capital of Jamestown, and they were free to move about the island. The older princes had each been allowed to bring one of their wives with them. The exiles were also accompanied by attendants and interpreters. During their exile, which lasted until 1897, a tutor was appointed to Dinuzulu, and he learned to read and write and to play the piano and organ. He spent much of his time riding horses and doing other physical activities. His uncles did not take up such European pursuits. Instead, they simply waited until the day they would be allowed to return home. For all their relative freedom, they were, after all, prisoners, forced to remain away from their homes and most of their relatives and other people who shared their language and culture.

WHILE IN EXILE ON THE ISLAND OF ST. HELENA, DINUZULU, SEATED IN WHITE HAT AND SUIT, SPENT TIME WITH HIS FAMILY, PICTURED. HE ALSO USED THIS TIME TO LEARN TO READ AND WRITE.

THE AFTERMATH OF THE ANGLO-ZULU WAR

Zibhebhu was also tried for his conduct and for the murder of an uSuthu headman (leader of a smaller group within the chiefdom). While he was acquitted (found innocent) and allowed to remain a chief, he was told that he could not return to Mandlakazi lands. Hostility between the uSuthu and the Mandlakazi continued to simmer. But the exile of Dinuzulu and the ban on Zibhebhu's return to his former lands reduced the threat of all-out war between the two groups.

ADMINISTRATIVE CHANGES AND NATURAL DISASTER

With the leaders of the warring factions in exile, Zululand experienced a few years of recovery. During this period, which began in 1890, the Zulu people could at last return to herding and farming. This provided some relief to those who had experienced food shortages throughout the years of war.

During this time of relative peace and stability, Britain made a series of changes in the region. On July 4, 1893, the British government granted Natal "responsible government" status. This meant that the Home Government would have less control over affairs in Natal and that the local colonial government would have greater authority and a greater degree of independence in ruling the land. Under this new status, British soldiers would remain in Natal for five years. After that time, they would leave, and Natal would be responsible for keeping order within its borders, without the assistance of the British military.

The British government also began to consider clemency (pardon) for the exiled Zulu princes. If granted, they would be allowed to return to Zululand.

Before the issue of clemency could be decided, however, locusts struck the region and destroyed crops. This led to famine (severe shortage of food). James Stuart, a British official who held various posts in Natal and Zululand, witnessed the 1895 famine. He wrote: "Immense clouds of [locusts] swept over the land in all directions, sometimes so vast as to render dimmer the light of the sun." The locusts continued to destroy crops each year until the early 1900s.

In addition to the locusts, 1896 brought a drought that killed thousands of cattle and many crops. On top of these problems, a new cattle disease washed through Zululand and Natal the next year. The disease, called rinderpest, killed many cattle. As a result of these disasters, the price of cattle increased by more than 500 percent. Zulu people, with diets that relied heavily on beef and milk, suffered from lack of food and from these increased costs. It became impossible for many young men to obtain cattle for lobolo (cattle given to the bride's family) , so they were unable to marry and start families.

PRESSING FOR ANNEXATION

Despite these problems, Natal continued to press for annexation of Zululand. Colonists in Natal hoped annexation would open the lands to white settlement and increase the colony's hut tax revenues. The British government finally granted permission in 1897, but with conditions. One of these created a five-year period during which land in Zululand would not be sold and local people would not be displaced without the British queen's approval. In the words of the official Act of Annexation, "until other provisions shall have been made . . . with the approval of Her Majesty, no grants or alienation [changing ownership] of Crown Lands [British lands]. . . shall be made, nor till then shall the Natives be disturbed in the use and occupation of any lands occupied or used by them at the time of the taking effect of this Act."

At nearly the same time, the British government had granted clemency to Dinuzulu, Ndabuko, and Shingana. It authorized their return to Zululand on the condition that Dinuzulu not be reinstated as king.

DINUZULU'S RETURN TO ZULULAND

Dinuzulu, Shingana, and Ndabuko arrived in Natal in early January 1898. Dinuzulu's official roles were to function as government induna and adviser and as chief over the uSuthu. After a few weeks at Eshowe, where he had been provided a house to conduct his affairs as government adviser, Dinuzulu returned to his people. He was welcomed back to the Ngome district with much enthusiasm. It was clear that, whatever his official status, many of the people still considered him a king. Two uSuthu regiments organized to build him a royal kraal named Usutu.

Dinuzulu preferred the comforts of home, and his unsupervised authority there, to his house and duties at Eshowe. At Usutu, he married several wives and took a dozen concubines (lovers he provided for, but did not marry). He began wearing a combination of European and Zulu clothing. His yearly salary from the British afforded him most of the luxuries he wanted, including European liquors. Fit and vigorous at the end of his exile, he grew so obese in the years after his return to Zululand that he had trouble moving about without help.

AFTER HIS RETURN FROM EXILE, DINUZULU WAS GIVEN A YEARLY SALARY BY THE BRITISH. HE USED THE MONEY TO BUY LUXURIES AND LIQUOR, WHICH CONTRIBUTED TO HIS PHYSICAL DETERIORATION IN LATER YEARS.

In January 1898, Zibhebhu was also allowed to return to his lands. For several years, it seemed that Zibhebhu and Dinuzulu would obey their strict orders not to resume their battle. Their feud revived briefly in 1904, when Zibhebhu demanded some cattle that he claimed Cetshwayo had owed him. Dinuzulu responded with a military buildup. However, before a confrontation could occur, Zibhebhu died on August 27, 1904.

TINDER FOR THE FLAMES OF REBELLION

As these events played out, other, more lasting changes were taking place in Zululand. These changes represented an upheaval in Zulu society in the aftermath of so many years of conflict. And this upheaval provided the tinder for rebellion.

Britain and the Boer Republics—the South African Republic and the Orange Free State—fought the Anglo-Boer War (also called the South African War) between 1899 and 1902. Though the main combatants considered this a "white man's war," many black Africans became involved in the fight. This war was extremely costly to Natal, both in terms of lives lost and money spent. Furthermore, the disruption to agriculture, combined with the droughts and cattle diseases spread poverty throughout the region.

The Anglo-Boer War ended in May 1902 with a British victory. In this war's aftermath, Natalians' interest in the fertile regions of Zululand grew. In 1903, five years after annexation, the Natal government opened these areas to white settlement. Less than half of the country, or about 3,887,000 acres (1,573,013 ha), was "reserved" exclusively for the use of local Africans. These plots were some of the worst land in Zululand. James Stuart described this land as "unsuitable for human habitation, either because of its being too arid [dry] and stony for cultivation, of malarial fever being prevalent [widespread] therein, or of its being infested with the tsetse fly [a disease-carrying fly]."

The Anglo-Boer War

THE ANGLO-BOER WAR, fought in southern Africa between Great Britain and the two Boer republics—the South African Republic and its ally the Orange Free State—broke out in 1899. The war began after a breakdown in negotiations over several issues. One of these issues was Britain's claim to a degree of authority over the South African Republic. (The 1881 treaty between the two countries had not granted the South African Republic complete independence.) Many British immigrants to the South African Republic were also working in the new city of Johannesburg, where gold had been discovered. Britain was concerned about the rights of British immigrants there. Britain had begun to negotiate with the South African Republic over these issues. But the negotiations failed on October 11, 1899, and the South African Republic and its allies went to war with the British.

At first, the local African people in the area were told that this conflict was a "white man's war." However, black African people did participate. As many as ten thousand armed African recruits served alongside British soldiers, performing duties such as scouting and guiding British troops. Perhaps as many as a hundred thousand also performed unarmed labor for the military on one side or the other.

The British took Pretoria, the capital of the South African Republic, in June 1900, but the war did not end there. Boer commandos continued to raid the British colonies of southern Africa, especially Cape Colony. The British responded by capturing Boer men and interning (imprisoning) women and children in concentration camps. In response to the Boers' tactics, the British attempted to cut off the Boers' supplies and authorized Dinuzulu to arm Zulu forces to defend themselves.

The man in charge of raiding Boer supply lines, Colonel Bottomley, appealed directly to Dinuzulu for help. Dinuzulu responded quickly, assembling about fifteen hundred men. Their raid was successful. Dinuzulu captured a Boer wagon and firearms and lost only two warriors. The raid was praised as having prevented a Boer attack, and its success contributed to Dinuzulu's standing in Zululand.

The treaty, called the Peace of Vereeniging, ended the Anglo-Boer War on May 31, 1902. Britain annexed the Boer republics, which became the Transvaal Colony and the Orange River Colony.

Concentration Camps

WHEN FIGHTING IN THE Anglo-Boer War continued even after the British took Pretoria in 1900, British military authorities in the region took drastic steps to try to end the fighting. Among these steps was the establishment of twenty-four camps in Natal and the Boer republics, supposedly for refugees from the war. British troops sent Boer women and children and noncombatant African families who worked for them to the camps by force. Altogether, by the end of the war, hundreds of thousands of Boer civilians and well over one hundred thousand black African civilians had been sent to the camps. These concentration camps consisted of crowded tents lacking in sufficient water or sanitation. The small rations of food that soldiers distributed contained little nutrition, and under such conditions, deadly diseases spread rapidly. An estimated 18,000 to 28,000 Boer women and children died in these concentration camps along with an estimated 12,000 or more Africans.

White settlers bought the newly opened land from the Natal government. Anyone (usually local Africans) who wanted to continue living on the land after it was purchased by the white settlers had to pay the new landlord rent. Some landlords charged rent in cash and others in service. Some of the landlords were more oppressive than others, but the local African people all considered the rents to be too high.

Cattle had been both the food and the currency in the nineteenth-century Zulu economy, and they remained central to the lives of most Zulu people. However, yet another disease, the East Coast Fever, or tick fever, had further reduced stock. The demands of cash for rent combined with the loss of so many cattle drove many people to borrow money. Opportunistic lenders took advantage of the situation. They charged interest on their loans, sometimes at exorbitant rates.

This maintained the cycle of poverty among black Africans in the aftermath of the Anglo-Zulu War.

Zulu culture faced dire consequences as a result of these events. In the nineteenth-century cultural system, the head of the household owned the household's cattle-wealth and was responsible for the members of his household. Sons cared for the cattle when they were young, and (until the system was abolished) joined a butho, a regiment for fighting or doing other work for the king or chief, when they grew older. In this system, young men were generally engaged in military training, war, and public works projects such as kraal building until they married and started their own households. Daughters provided additional hands in the gardens and fields until they married. At that time, the father received cattle as lobolo in exchange for the loss of their labor.

In the new era of colonial dominance, Zulu families required cash for food, rents, and repayment of debts. Many young men, unable to buy enough cattle for lobolo, went off to work elsewhere. Many ended up taking manual jobs in and around the white-owned gold mines in Johannesburg and Barberton. Their wages became the main source of income for households back home and at the same time led to a new sense of independence among young Zulu men. This independence caused a rift in many families. Men who went to the mines stayed there for months out of the year. Their wages were paid to them directly, which their fathers resented. Sometimes the young men spent a large portion of the money in southern African mining towns rather than sending the money back to their families, who depended on this source of income.

The aftermath of the years of war and conflict and the imposition of European dominance further weakened the earlier cultural bonds of Zulu society. For example, the chiefdom ceased to be the primary unit of community and family identification for this generation of young Zulu men. At the mines, new bonds of community were created at the workplace among the laborers, who came from all over southern Africa and elsewhere. Race awareness and hostility between blacks and whites also increased. For example, work at the racially segregated mines increased resentment against the white mine operators, resentment that easily and naturally extended to the white landlords at home. These factors led to a greater suspicion between black and white people in Natal. More people, both black and white, began to see black and white, rather than British or Boer, Zulu or other African ethnicities, as a fundamental political and cultural distinction.

IN THE EARLY 1900S, MANY ZULUS TOOK MANUAL JOBS IN THE WHITE-OWNED GOLD MINES OF JOHANNESBURG.

THE AFTERMATH OF THE ANGLO-ZULU WAR

THE CENSUS

In 1904 the Natal colonial authorities increased Zulu suspicions by conducting a census in Natal and Zululand. It was common practice in British colonies to count all residents, including local people. However, this had never been done in Zululand. Many Zulu residents had heard a rumor that the purpose of the census was to discover how many cattle the Zulu people had so that white people could take them away. They also feared that the census would be used to gain more tax money from the locals.

These concerns led one Zulu chief to speak out against the census. In April 1904, Bhambatha, chief of the Zondi chiefdom, brought his people before J. W. Cross, the magistrate of the Umvoti district where they lived, to pay their hut taxes. Cross asked them to give information for the census. Bhambatha protested and concluded his comments with the words "If there be anything behind all this, we shall be angry."

Cross tried to reassure him: "You may as well expect the sun to fall from the heavens as imagine that harm will come to you."

"That was just what we wanted to hear," Bhambatha replied.

THE POLL TAX

In fact, as many Zulu people suspected, the Natal government followed up the census with a new tax. The Anglo-Boer War had drained Natal's treasury, and the colonial government needed cash to help pay off debts. In August 1905, the Natal legislature passed a Poll Tax Law that placed a tax upon each unmarried man. Those who were already subject to the hut tax were exempt from (did not have to pay) the poll tax. This meant that most young men had to pay the poll tax, and older men paid the hut tax.

Reactions among the Zulu chiefs ranged from minor regret to vehement protests. Resentment arose not only because of the fact the people were being required to pay an additional tax, but also because the chiefs had been promised that the census would not be used to do them injury. Furthermore, claimed some Zulu headmen, "the law would result in complete loss of the small control kraal-owners still retained over their sons," because being taxed separately from their fathers' households further increased the young men's independence.

Bhambatha reminded Cross of his words the previous April and asked him to explain. Though he tried, the magistrate was unable to do so to Bhambatha's satisfaction.

> *The Natives of India [a British colony at the time] are governed and treated in a correct manner [by Britain], and according to the law . . . but we who were subdued . . . are not treated in the same manner as they have been treated. The laws are not the same. We cannot help feeling that we Zulu people have been discriminated against."*
>
> —Dinuzulu, ca. 1906

Dinuzulu, on the other hand, did not protest the tax. Contrary to rumors that he was planning to rebel against the white authorities, he paid his tax early. This encouraged many of the other chiefs to make sure that their people paid their taxes, which would begin to be collected on January 20, 1906. Not all of the chiefs paid, though. According to Stuart,

THE AFTERMATH OF THE ANGLO-ZULU WAR

UNMARRIED ZULU MEN MEET WITH COLONIAL ADMINISTRATORS TO PAY POLL TAXES, WHICH WERE PASSED INTO LAW BY THE NATAL LEGISLATURE IN AUGUST 1905.

some of them "appeared to be offering a passive resistance [a nonviolent form of protest]," while others resorted to violent demonstrations.

War and famine had increased poverty in Zululand. Colonization had made it worse by forcing Zulu families onto poor land or requiring them to pay rents. A previously unheard-of and feared census had been conducted in spite of the chiefs' objections. On top of these misfortunes, the white colonial authorities had imposed a new tax, which fell largely on the shoulders of young, unmarried men. The many changes in Zulu society in the aftermath of Natal's annexation of Zululand had left young Zulu men independent, unattached to the households of their fathers or to new households of their own. Even if the rumors that Dinuzulu was about to lead these men in a rebellion against colonial rule were untrue, rebellion was imminent.

CHAPTER 7

Zululand's Final Throes

THE ANGLO-ZULU WAR of 1879 and its aftermath set in motion a series of changes that forever altered life for the Zulu people. These changes eventually resulted in government by white colonial authorities, with Zulu lands restricted to reserves and subject to colonial laws and taxes.

The changes moved at a slow, steady pace. More than twenty-five years after the war, many Zulu loyalists still saw Dinuzulu as their king. Many also resented the colonial authority's growing control of Zulu life and property. These factors—along with growing racial tension, poverty, and a large number of angry young men free from family ties—led to increasing tensions between some Zulu groups and the British authorities. With the implementation of the poll tax, these tensions exploded.

Incident at Trewirgie

The poll tax triggered protests all across Zululand as collection began in January and February 1906. Anger threatened to turn some protests into violent confrontations. At Maphumulo (in what is modern-day KwaZulu-Natal, South Africa), for instance, three hundred men armed with shields, sticks, and knobkerries (wooden war clubs with long handles and round heads) surrounded the magistate who had come to collect the tax. When he tried to speak to them, they shouted "Shut up! we refuse to pay!" The mob threateningly shook their sticks at him but went no further.

ALL OVER ZULULAND, THE LOCAL PEOPLE BECAME RESENTFUL OF THE GROWING CONTROL OF COLONIAL AUTHORITIES AND OF COLONIAL LAW. THEY BEGAN ORGANIZING PROTESTS AGAINST THE POLL TAX AS COLLECTION BEGAN IN EARLY 1906.

Other protests brought real violence. On February 7, the magistrate of the Umgeni district went to an area near Pietermaritzburg to collect taxes. Before he reached his destination, a local chief named Mveli warned him about a group of armed men who were waiting to confront the tax collector. A soldier sent to investigate discovered a group of twenty-seven young Zulu men, most of whom carried assegais. Having lost the element of surprise, they threatened the soldier, but the confrontation ended there. The colonial government did not let the matter die, however. Authorities issued arrest warrants against the twenty-seven men for "taking part in an assembly of armed men without the authority of the Supreme Chief," an act prohibited by the Code of Native Law.

About a dozen policemen, led by District Police Sub-Inspector Sidney H. K. Hunt, traveled for most of the next day to serve the warrants. The men were said to be hiding in kraals near a white colonist's farm called Trewirgie. As the police approached Trewirgie, at first they found only women and old men in the kraals. With the help of one of the old men, they finally located and arrested three of the suspects, including an older man named Mjongo who was their leader. A short time later, the police discovered that the suspects had gathered on a nearby hill, joined by dozens of other men armed with assegais and knobkerries. Hunt and two other officers confronted the men, wanting to know what they were doing there.

"You have come for our money; you can shoot us; we refuse to pay," they shouted. They shook their assegais and knobkerries but backed up the hill as Hunt and his men pressed forward. At this point, Hunt released Mjongo, hoping that he would be able to reduce the tension. It did not work out that way. The mob grabbed Mjongo and pulled him away from the police and into the midst of the group. The police retreated downhill, and the shouting group of young men advanced.

The police were about to retreat with their two prisoners when the men charged at them and tried to rescue their comrades. By this time, it had gotten dark and the air was misty. A struggle ensued, and Hunt fired his revolver into the air. At the sound of the gunshot, the fight turned bloody. The rebels began to use their assegais, and the police, their guns. Hunt and another officer were killed, each stabbed more than a dozen times. A third officer was wounded. The other police fled, and the young men did the same, making their way into the nearby Enon forest.

GOVERNMENT RESPONSE

Up to this point, all of the armed demonstrations had opposed only the tax and focused just on government representatives. No actions had been taken against the colony's white settlers. Even so, settlers in many areas began to panic, fearing a general rebellion against all whites. The white family living at Trewirgie, for instance, fled to Pietermaritzburg. Rumors flew that black residents were talking about killing the whites and that Dinuzulu or some other Zulu leader was about to stage a large-scale rebellion. It seemed to many white residents that the race war they had long predicted was about to ignite.

Because of these fears, white residents of Natal-Zululand supported a swift, decisive reaction to the incident at Trewirgie. Natal authorities mobilized the militia and declared martial law (military control of the country during an emergency). Around one thousand militiamen converged on Trewirgie to search for the armed protesters.

Within days, they found two of the men. Both were tried by a military tribunal (military court). They were found guilty of participating in the murder of the policemen and sentenced to die. The execution, by

International Reaction to the Trewirgie Courts-Martial

ON MARCH 27, 1906, word of the sentences for the Trewirgie incident reached Lord Elgin, secretary of state for the colonies, in London. Elgin asked the Natalian officials to suspend (delay) the death sentences until he could review them. As his telegram stated, "Continued executions under martial law [are] certain to excite strong criticism here" and "civil courts [are] greatly to be preferred."

Vocal protests of Elgin's request came from not only Natal but from such far-flung parts of the British Empire as Australia and New Zealand. As a result, Elgin gave in, telling the government of Natal that the members of the British goverment "have at no time had the intention to interfere with action of the responsible government of Natal. . . . In the light of the information now furnished, His Majesty's [Edward VII, who succeeded Queen Victoria in 1901] Government recognize that the decision of this grave matter rests in the hands of your Ministers and yourself."

LORD ELGIN, RIGHT, ASKED NATAL OFFICIALS TO DELAY THE DEATH SENTENCES HANDED OUT IN THE TREWIRGIE COURTS-MARTIAL.

gunshot, took place that same day, on February 15, 1906. Word spread quickly about the strict sentence.

The militia troops then put Mveli in charge of capturing the rest of these men they considered rebels. Some of the rebels died attacking

Mveli's men, but many more were captured. Between February 22 and March 19, the military authorities in Natal carried out many courts-martial (military trials). Most of the captives who were tried were found guilty. Sentences ranged from fines, to lashes, to execution. Twelve of the participants in the fight at Trewirgie were sentenced to death for the murder of the policemen, and they stood before a firing squad on April 2.

The executions probably deterred some of the people who might have rebelled. But in some cases, they had the opposite effect. When rumors began to fly that certain chiefs were going to be arrested, they began to arm their men out of fear of execution.

BHAMBATHA

One of these accidental rebels was Bhambatha. He had spoken out against the tax and certainly did not want to pay it, but, powerless, he prepared to pay anyway. He assembled his men on February 22, the day he had been ordered to appear at Cross's office in Greytown to pay the tax.

However, Bhambatha did not make it to the magistrate's office. A few miles from Greytown, he discovered that Nhlonhlo, one of his headmen who strongly opposed the tax, had assembled a number of young men armed with shields and assegais. They refused to disarm and go to pay the tax. Furthermore, some of Bhambatha's men who had not armed with Nhlonhlo's group had not brought enough money for their taxes. Bhambatha began to fear that he might be punished or even executed for the men's lack of money, for being late for his meeting with Cross, and for the fact that some of his men had armed illegally. So instead of appearing in person, he sent a representative to the magistrate to say that he was sick.

For his failure to show up before Cross and pay his taxes, Bhambatha was summoned by the authorities. In the meantime, he stayed with Nhlonhlo and his armed men. Nhlonhlo further convinced Bhambatha that the authorities would consider him to be a rebel and would arrest him for staying with the illegally armed group. When Bhambatha did not show up for this meeting either, the authorities officially replaced him as chief.

The authorities then sent a large police force to arrest Bhambatha on March 9. But he remained in hiding, feeling he had no choice but to rebel or be arrested and possibly executed. He told his men that the next time they saw him, he would be leading an army. He then fled from Umvoti.

BHAMBATHA AND DINUZULU

Many Zulu people still regarded Dinuzulu as their king. He was the most influential figure among the local African population of the Natal colony. Rumors flew that he was planning to rise up and force the white colonists to leave Zululand. Any rebellion headed by Dinuzulu would receive widespread support. Since Bhambatha had decided to rebel, he planned to enlist Dinuzulu's support.

Bhambatha, along with some of his family, eventually made his way to Dinuzulu's Usutu kraal on the Zululand side of the colony. Dinuzulu (who was ill and bedridden at this time) met with Bhambatha and treated him well, inviting his wife and family to stay at Usutu. However, he gave no clear sign of support.

This lack of immediate public support did not trouble Bhambatha. He used Dinuzulu's friendly reception to make it appear that he was operating under Dinuzulu's orders. This appearance of support grew when two of Dinuzulu's closest associates accompanied Bhambatha back to the Mpanza Valley on the Natal side of the colony. One of them, Cakijana, was widely known as Dinuzulu's personal attendant. The official purpose of this escort was to make sure Bhambatha left Zululand to prevent him from causing trouble for Dinuzulu. The other purpose was to bring a famous Zulu doctor back to Dinuzulu to help treat his illness.

ONSET OF REBELLION

Bhambatha arrived back in the Mpanza Valley on March 31, 1906, and began to raise an army of young men. Cakijana believed that Dinuzulu's real motive for sending him with Bhambatha was to support the rebellion. So he helped gather fighters. These rebels began harassing government officials and troops with some success.

In a surprise attack on April 3, armed with rifles and assegais, they engaged the magistrate and the five other men who accompanied him. A column of soldiers was sent in response. As they escorted the

A British Officer at Mpanza

"WHEN THE [ZULU] REBELS STARTED their attack, they volleyed [shot] into us; as they did so, the majority, with assegais, sprang on to the road to stab, or throw where that was impossible. . . . The practically simultaneous wounding of many horses caused them, as well as others, to plunge about. During the resulting confusion, the guard, as the attack was being delivered, was pressed forward. I suddenly hear Trumpeter Milton on my left cry out. He had been struck in the back by, I believe, a flung assegai. . . . I told the men, about eight or ten of them, to bunch together, when we began to work our way back. The enemy at this time was in the bush on both sides of the road, being briskly fired at by the main body."

—Major O. Dimmick, officer in command of the advance
guard at the April 1906 Mpanza Valley attack

magistrate's party out of the Mpanza Valley during the night, about 150 of the rebels, led by Bhambatha and Cakijana, attacked. The rebels took up the royal cry of "uSuthu!" as they attacked. They managed to kill four of the soldiers and wound four more. Around a dozen of the rebels were wounded, but none killed. This was because the soldiers were mostly firing blindly into the forest. The rebels were able to crawl through the brush and avoid being hit by the bullets that whizzed overhead.

In spite of that success, Bhambatha gained little support from the chiefs in Natal. As more government forces converged on the Mpanza Valley, he recrossed the Tugela River into Zululand. He and his men made for the Nkandhla forest and the lands of elderly Sigananda, a chief who was very loyal to Dinuzulu. Sigananda's people had taken part in protests against the colonial authorities. As a result, authorities had started proceedings to remove Sigananda from his chieftainship. Bhambatha hoped to gain his support by claiming that he was acting on the king's behalf.

Dinuzulu continued to officially denounce the rebellion, offering to send out his men against Bhambatha. He also sent messengers to inform Sigananda of his opposition. But the rebels successfully convinced Sigananda that the king actually wanted him to rebel and turned away any messenger who bore news to the contrary.

Fast Fact

During the period of raids and counterraids between government forces and Bhambatha's men in April and May 1906, the government forces issued calico or red armbands to "loyal" Zulu fighters to wear as a way to distinguish them from the Zulu rebels. The armbands were later replaced with headbands, which were easier to see.

With the support of this respected chief and many of his men, Bhambatha's forces began to grow more quickly. They supplied themselves by looting stores and raiding the kraals of Zulu men who refused to join the rebellion.

At the beginning of May, government forces began sending out reconnaissance (scouting) missions. They burned kraals and seized cattle where they discovered that rebels had been obtaining food or shelter. Skirmishes took place in which a few rebels were killed and artillery fired, but no major engagements occurred until May 5.

THE BOBE ENGAGEMENT

Bhambatha won Sigananda's support. And many Zulu people believed that Dinuzulu was secretly behind him. But many also questioned Bhambatha's leadership skills. Without a trusted leader, the rebellion that Bhambatha hoped to carry out could not succeed.

On May 5, 1906, about one thousand of Bhambatha's rebels encountered government forces numbering around nine hundred men. The troops were scouting and burning kraals in a valley south of the Nkandhla forest at the foot of a ridge called Bobe. The rebels were divided into several groups. The first group to encounter the government forces jumped up and attacked, shouting "uSuthu!" A few times they came close enough for hand-to-hand combat, but they were soon scattered by superior numbers and firepower.

Another group of about four hundred men, led by Bhambatha himself, approached the rear guard (the soldiers guarding the back of the column) late in the day but held back. The government soldiers were tired. Since they had only come to survey the area, they did not attack and retreated instead. The rebels followed and kept up a constant sniper fire during the night but did not launch another full-scale attack.

BHAMBATHA'S FIGHTERS CLASH WITH GOVERNMENT FORCES ON MAY 5, 1906. THIS MID-TWENTIETH-CENTURY PAINTING OF THE BOBE ENGAGEMENT IS BY JAMES EDWIN McCONNELL.

Altogether, sixty to seventy rebels were killed in the engagement and many wounded. Only one Natal reserve and one Zululand policeman were wounded.

The Bobe engagement represented a setback to Bhambatha as a leader. One way he had convinced men to fight for him was by claiming that magic would keep the white men's bullets from striking the flesh of those fighting in his righteous cause. The fact that he did not follow up the government soldiers' retreat with a full-scale attack made it seem that he was, however, actually afraid of those bullets.

THE MOME GORGE

Even with the May 5 setback, rebel forces continued to grow. They gathered near the Mome Gorge near modern-day Nkandla, KwaZulu-Natal, South Africa. There, government forces tried several times to attack them. Bhambatha usually managed to learn about the attacks and slip away with his forces without a major engagement. This was not always the case, though. Some larger skirmishes resulted in many rebel deaths. One such skirmish took place on May 27, when about eight hundred rebels attacked a military camp at Mpukunyoni. More than one hundred rebels died under fire. However, no clear winner came out of these encounters.

On the night of June 9, Colonel Duncan McKenzie, who was in charge of the combined government forces massed against the rebels, learned of Bhambatha's location. He also learned when and where his forces would be moving through the Mome Gorge. McKenzie immediately sent out his troops to surround the rebels in the Mome Valley. They had to move quickly and quietly in the night and were not to fire a shot before the attack at daybreak. Despite fears that moving the big guns into position would give away their location, they surrounded the rebel army without being heard.

At dawn, artillery and rifle bullets began raining down into the valley from the ridges. One apparent means of escape, the Dobo forest, was left open and many of the rebels fled there. However, at 9:00 A.M., the artillerymen sent up a shower of shells throughout the forest. A large group of McKenzie's troops then combed the forest to drive any survivors back into the Mome Valley. Some did escape, but more than five hundred rebels were killed in the action. Although it was not known until several days later, Bhambatha was among the dead. Casualties among McKenzie's men were light. With superior weapons and a good field position, government soldiers suffered only three deaths and a few more injuries.

The battle at the Mome Gorge marked the turning point in the rebellion. This was the last major action for the rebels in Zululand. By the middle of July, the rebellion in Natal had also concluded.

Altogether, more than 10,000 residents of the Zululand-Natal region rebelled in 1906. More than 2,000 of them were killed and many more wounded. The government took about 4,700 prisoners, most of whom were convicted of participating in the rebellion by military courts. Among the organized, well-armed government troops, twenty-four white and six African soldiers were killed or died of wounds. Sixty-seven more were wounded.

The Trial of Dinuzulu

During the rebellion, government officials accepted Dinuzulu's claim that he opposed Bhambatha's actions. However, a large group of Natalian officials wanted to eliminate any chance of the monarchy's revival. They saw Dinuzulu as a potential threat to white authority in the colony. So in the aftermath of Bhambatha's rebellion, they accused Dinuzulu of various crimes including sheltering some of the rebels at his Usutu kraal. They used these charges to bring Dinuzulu to trial.

Supporters of Dinuzulu accused the government of rigging the trial against him. In fact, the original primary defense attorney, E. G. Jellico from England, refused to participate in the case. He claimed that the defense was not allowed to gather evidence that would support Dinuzulu and that witness testimony had been doctored (changed). During these preliminary examinations, one of the defense attorneys, Robert Charles Azariah

WITNESSES AGAINST DINUZULU IN HIS TRIAL FOR TREASON POSED FOR THIS PHOTOGRAPH IN 1908.

Samuelson, reported that the witnesses had to sit facing away from Dinuzulu. When Jellico objected, the presiding officer of the court told him that if he did "not shut up he would be bundled out with all his papers."

Nevertheless, Dinuzulu's accusers were unable to make many of their charges stick. Of the twenty-three charges brought against him, Dinuzulu was found guilty of only two—high treason for harboring Bhambatha's family at Usutu and for harboring and assisting Bhambatha and other rebels when they visited Usutu during the rebellion. He was fined and sentenced to a four-year prison term.

> *The only safe course [for the British] is to close our eyes to the colour of the natives and give them unstinted [complete] justice and fair play free of any differentiation against them; extend to them sympathy and kindness. . . . All will be well for Africa if right is done and all wrong if wrong is done."*
>
> —Defense attorney for Dinuzulu, Robert Charles Azariah Samuelson, 1929

"UP FROM THE SEA"

With the rebellion quashed and the former king in prison, hopes for an independent Zulu nation died. White control of Zulu lands would be realized in full.

As he was being assassinated in 1828, Shaka, the mighty founder of the Zulu kingdom, is reported to have told his brothers, "Your country, children of my father, will be ruled by white people who will come up from the sea." At the turn of the century, his prophecy had come to pass.

South Africa in the Twentieth Century

N 1909, REPRESENTATIVES from the four South African colonies—Cape Colony, the Orange River Colony, Transvaal, and Natal—met to write a constitution for a new union. In all four colonies, white males dominated the government (although some additional racial groups could vote in Cape Colony). In spite of their differences, both Afrikaners (speakers of Afrikaans, or African Dutch, generally descendants of Dutch colonists) and British residents supported union. The 1909 South Africa Act, approved by the British government, made the union official. On May 31, 1910, Afrikaner Louis Botha became the first prime minister of the Union of South Africa. Within this union lived a total of about 1,275,000 white people, mostly of British and Afrikaner descent, 4,000,000 black Africans, 500,000 coloreds (the term applied in South Africa to people of mixed white and black heritage), and 150,000 people of Indian descent. (Indians had come to southern Africa since the

1860s as laborers working in the British Empire, which also included India at that time.)

Botha had been one of the Boers who had joined Dinuzulu in the 1884 attack on Zibhebhu and looked upon Dinuzulu as a friend. He therefore released Dinuzulu from prison and gave him a farm in the Transvaal, where he lived out his few remaining years.

During much of the first half of the twentieth century, tensions between the two politically dominant South African ethnic groups, the Afrikaners and the English-speaking British descendants, were common. In addition, the white minority government took stronger and stronger measures over time to maintain political and economic dominance over the nation's nonwhite majority. Gradually, laws were put into place to increase the forced and legal separation of the races and to further restrict the movement and opportunities for nonwhites. For example, in 1913, the Natives Land Act prohibited black Africans from buying land outside the reserves, which constituted only 7 percent of the country (and was increased to just 13 percent in 1926). The act also prohibited black people from renting farmland for themselves outside the reserves. They could work only on white-owned lands as laborers.

LOUIS BOTHA BECAME THE FIRST PRIME MINISTER OF THE UNION OF SOUTH AFRICA ON MAY 31, 1910.

The Adoption of Apartheid

After World War II (1939–1945), a new political coalition (group of people from different political parties) took control of the South African government in 1948. The political slogan that won the day was an Afrikaans word—apartheid—meaning "separateness" (of the races). Apartheid came to be the name for the South African system of legal racial segregation, which endured for decades.

In 1949 came the Mixed Marriage Act, which prohibited people of different races from marrying. This was followed in 1950 by the Population Registration Act, which required everyone in South Africa to register as black, white, Asian, or colored. The legislature and courts continued to increase the legal segregation of the races throughout the 1950s.

Over the years, black South Africans held protests and demonstrations. In 1960, during a particularly massive—though peaceful—protest, police at Sharpeville shot into the unarmed crowd, killing more than sixty people and injuring more than one hundred. The government went on to ban all black political organizations, including the African National Congress (ANC), a group working for the peaceful restoration of rights to black South Africans. In response to these events of 1960, organizations like the ANC had to go underground (operate in secret). Since they could no longer protest peacefully for fear of violent government response, their leaders decided that they had no choice but to develop military wings.

The ruling minority sought to further divide and weaken South Africa's black population. In the 1970s, black residents had to register as one of around ten different groups and to move to a "homeland" reserved for their group. Black Africans who went to cities outside their "homelands" needed special permission on an official document, or pass, to stay for more than seventy-two hours. If they did not have a pass, they could be arrested. Most black African groups opposed the establishment of the homelands. One, however, did not. These were some of the Zulu people who hoped to revive the Zulu nation. In KwaZulu, the area reserved for the Zulu people, arose the Inkatha, an organization dedicated to reviving Zulu culture.

Inkatha, led by Chief Mangosuthu Buthelezi, gained the support of many rural and conservative people in KwaZulu and Natal, while many other Zulu people, especially those who lived in the cities, supported other groups like the ANC. Most of these other groups working for black rights tried to unify the different ethnic groups in their struggle. Inkatha, however, was concerned only with the Zulu nation and culture. Violent fights frequently erupted between groups of Inkatha supporters and supporters of other black South African movements.

In the 1970s, Zulu chief Mangosuthu Buthelezi led Inkatha, an organization dedicated to reviving Zulu culture and ending apartheid.

THE END OF APARTHEID

In the 1980s, it had become increasingly evident that apartheid could no longer work. Black governments had come to power in neighboring African countries formerly controlled by European colonies. Unrest at home, including protests and labor strikes, continued to increase and crippled the nation. South Africa had become an outcast in the international community, subject to punitive trade bans and restrictions. In response, a new constitution was created in 1984 that gave a very limited increase in political freedom to colored and Asian people, though not to black South Africans.

Momentous change was in the air when in 1990, South African president Frederik Willem de Klerk lifted bans against the ANC and other African political groups. He also released political prisoners. One, an ANC leader named Nelson Mandela, had spent nearly thirty years in prison. After Mandela's release in 1990, he and de Klerk worked together to establish a convention that would create a new constitution. In 1991 the convention began the work of creating a new constitution to end the apartheid system and to create a nonracial system of government in South Africa. The nation's first free and open nonracial elections were scheduled to be held in 1994.

The country teetered on the brink of civil war during the process of dismantling apartheid from 1990 to 1994, and obstacles to the creation of the new constitution arose on all sides. One of these obstacles included a challenge by the Inkatha Freedom Party (IFP). This party represented conservative Zulu people and Zulu king Goodwill Zwelithini. It demanded an independent Zulu kingdom consisting of all of the land conquered by Shaka. Headed by Chief Buthelezi, the prime minister of KwaZulu, the IFP presented a powerful rival to the ANC in KwaZulu and Natal, although many urban Zulu people continued to support the ANC.

In 1990 fighting broke out in Natal between IFP and ANC supporters, resulting in hundreds of deaths. Sporadic violence continued, with the IFP promising to boycott (not take part in) elections. Mandela and de Klerk ultimately made a secret deal with the king to give him 3 million acres (1.2 million ha) of land. One week before the elections in 1994, the IFP agreed to participate.

In 1994 Nelson Mandela became president of South Africa in the nation's first election open to South Africans of all backgrounds. He began the work of healing a country torn by decades of apartheid. The transition was accompanied by violence, yet all-out civil war never came to pass. This amazing feat led to a 1993 Nobel Peace Prize shared between Mandela and de Klerk.

NELSON MANDELA, CENTER, AND SOUTH AFRICAN PRESIDENT F. W. DE KLERK, RIGHT, DISPLAY THE 1993 NOBEL PEACE PRIZE THAT THEY JOINTLY SHARED FOR THEIR EFFORTS TO END APARTHEID IN SOUTH AFRICA.

South Africa in the Twenty-First Century

South Africa is the wealthiest country in Africa. It is the largest producer of gold and platinum and has many other natural resources. Its financial and industrial systems are advanced, and the nation has highly functioning systems of transportation and delivery of services. However, it continues to face daunting challenges to address the AIDS pandemic (worldwide outbreak) and the problems created by the years of unequal education, health care, job opportunities, and living standards under apartheid.

Modern KwaZulu-Natal

The Zulu royal line continued after Dinuzulu's death in 1913 with his son Nkayishana, or Solomon. The head of the Zulu royal household maintained prestige even though the kingship was abolished. In 1952 Britain again recognized the head of the house of Zulu, then Nkayishana's son, Bhekuzulu (Cyprian), as paramount (head) chief of the Zulu people. (Dinuzulu was officially chief of only the uSuthu.) Goodwill Zwelithini, Bhekuzulu's eldest son, became the eighth Zulu king in 1971. He continues to reign in the twenty-first century, although his official position in South Africa is largely ceremonial and advisory to the provincial government of KwaZulu-Natal.

In modern South Africa, KwaZulu-Natal is one of the nation's nine provinces. In 2006 the province observed the one-hundred-year anniversary of the Bhambatha Rebellion and launched a campaign to commemorate the Zulu people's heritage by remembering the wars of resistance fought by Kings Cetshwayo and Dinuzulu. As a part of this movement, Bhambatha was posthumously (after death) reinstated as chief of the Zondi. This was a symbolic gesture to recognize the courage of all the Africans of what became KwaZulu-Natal who stood up to the colonial oppressors in 1906.

Furthermore, the sacred eMakhosini Valley, so long in the hands of white farmers, is being acquired by the provincial government. It will eventually become a heritage park as a memorial to Zulu history.

The Anglo-Zulu War of 1879 set in motion the events that would make Zululand a part of a white European colony. In the aftermath of that war, white rule was gradually expanded in the colony to prevent the kingdom's revival. Yet neither the war nor its powerful aftermath erased Zulu identity, and Zulu language and culture remain strong. In the twenty-first century, in the aftermath of the historic struggle between European colonial forces and the local inhabitants of southern Africa, the Zulu people are now one part of a larger multicultural, multiracial democratic and independent South Africa.

Timeline

1816	Shaka seizes the Zulu chieftainship.
1824	The Natal settlement is created, with Shaka's permission, to trade in the region of southeastern Africa.
September 24, 1828	Shaka is assassinated and Dingane seizes power.
1835	The Great Trek begins.
1840	Mpande's army, supported by Boers, defeats Dingane. Mpande gives control of Natal to the Boers living there.
1842	The British conquer Natal. Mpande allows some Boers to settle in Zululand as far east as Utrecht (in what is modern-day Utrecht, KwaZulu-Natal, South Africa).
1856	Supporters of Mbuyazi and of Cetshwayo battle for the Zulu kingship. Cetshwayo's victory ensures his succession.
October 1872	Mpande dies.
1873	Cetshwayo formally becomes Zulu king.
1877	The British Empire annexes the Transvaal.
1878	The Sihayo and Middle Drift affairs occur. Shepstone delivers Frere's ultimatum to Cetshwayo's chiefs on December 11.

January 11, 1879	Chelmsford crosses the Buffalo River into Zululand with the main British invasion forces.
January 22, 1879	Zulu army soundly defeats British forces remaining encamped at Isandhlwana.
July 4, 1879	The British defeat the main Zulu army at the Battle of Ulundi.
August 28, 1879	Cetshwayo is captured by the British, to be exiled in Cape Colony.
September 1, 1879	The Wolseley plan is announced to the Zulu chiefs, and Zululand is divided into thirteen independent chiefdoms.
1880	uSuthu deputations protest Zibhebhu's, Hamu's, and Dunn's behavior and request the return of Cetshwayo as king. Protests continue into 1882.
March 1881	The South African Republic (Transvaal) regains independence.
August 3, 1882	Cetshwayo arrives in England to plead his case to be allowed to return to Zululand.
January 29, 1883	Cetshwayo is reinstalled as Zulu king.
March 30, 1883	Ndabuko takes an army to attack Zibhebhu but is defeated.
July 21, 1883	Zibhebhu attacks Ulundi and wipes out many Zulu leaders.
February 8, 1884	Cetshwayo dies.
June 5, 1884	Zibhebhu's forces are defeated at the Battle of Tshaneni by uSuthu forces backed up by one hundred Boers.

August 16, 1884	Dinuzulu signs a treaty that grants the land for the New Republic to his Boer supporters.
October 26, 1885	The New Republic claims additional land from Zululand.
October 22, 1886	The New Republic and British authorities agree to a reduced territory for the New Republic.
February–May 1887	The British Empire annexes Zululand.
September 14, 1887	The New Republic merges with the South African Republic.
November 14, 1887	The British inform Dinuzulu that he cannot rule as king in Zululand.
June 2, 1888	Dinuzulu's forces clash with British colonial government forces at Ceza Mountain, forcing the government troops to retreat.
June 23, 1888	Dinuzulu's army defeats Zibhebhu at Ivuna.
September 11, 1888	Dinuzulu surrenders himself to the South African Republic.
November 12, 1888	The British arrest Dinuzulu at Bishopstowe.
February–April 1889	Dinuzulu, Ndabuko, and Shingana are tried and found guilty of various crimes, including high treason.
1890	Dinuzulu, Ndabuko, and Shingana are exiled on the island of St. Helena until 1897.
July 4, 1893	Britain grants Natal "responsible government" status, giving the local colonial government greater authority and a greater degree of independence in ruling the land.

1895	A series of misfortunes such as drought, plagues of locusts, and cattle diseases begins to ravage Zululand and Natal for several years.
1897	Natal annexes Zululand.
January 1898	Dinuzulu returns to Zululand as government induna and uSuthu chief.
1899	The Anglo-Boer War begins between Britain and the South African Republic allied with the Orange Free State. Britain conquers the republics in 1902.
1903	The land in Zululand, except for areas reserved for local African use, is opened to white settlement.
1904	British colonial authorities conduct a census in Zululand.
August 27, 1904	Zibhebhu dies.
1905	Natal institutes a poll tax.
February 8, 1906	Two police officers are killed at Trewirgie by protesters who refused to pay the poll tax.
March–July 1906	Rebels led by Bhambatha hold out against Natalian colonial police and militia soldiers in a widespread rebellion.
June 9, 1906	Bhambatha and more than five hundred rebels are killed by government troops in the Mome Gorge.
December 7, 1907	Dinuzulu is arrested for alleged participation in the rebellion.

1909	The Union of South Africa is created, merging Natal with Cape Colony, the Orange River Colony, and the Transvaal.
1913	The Natives Land Act prohibits Africans from buying land outside the reserves.
1960	Police shoot into a crowd demonstrating for black South African rights in Sharpeville, South Africa, killing sixty-seven and wounding many more. The incident sparks widespread outrage. In an effort to stem resulting disturbances, the South African government bans organizations such as the African National Congress, which work for racial political equality in South Africa.
1961	South Africa ceases to be a part of the British Commonwealth.
1990	South African president Frederik Willem de Klerk lifts the ban on black political organizations.
1994	South Africa's first nonracial election is held. Nelson Mandela becomes South Africa's first black president.

Glossary

Afrikaner: a South African descendant of European settlers who speaks Afrikaans, or African Dutch; usually a descendant of Dutch colonists in South Africa. Cape Colony was founded in the south-western tip of southern Africa by the Dutch in 1652, and over time, these colonists evolved their own unique culture and language (Afrikaans).

annexation: to make another political entity, such as a country, part of one's own; for example, when Natal annexed Zululand, Zululand became a part of Natal

assegai: an iron-tipped spear, a common weapon in southeastern Africa in the nineteenth century

Boer: a Dutch-speaking white farmer in southern Africa, especially one living in the Transvaal or a nearby region

butho: a group of men or women gathered by a Zulu chief or king to be trained for war and/or to be used for the completion of public works projects such as the building of royal kraals or raising crops

commando: a group of mounted soldiers armed with guns for quick offensive maneuvers

drift: an area where the water is shallow enough for wagons to cross

exile: to send someone away from his/her homeland as a punishment

impi: a Zulu army or regiment of soldiers

isiZulu: the Zulu language

kraal: the Zulu homestead formed by a circle of huts surrounding a cattle enclosure

laager: a fortified area where people inside can fire outward in all directions, especially a ring of ox-drawn carriages such as those used by the Trekkers to defend themselves when facing an enemy

lobolo: part of the nineteenth-century Zulu economy in which cattle are given to the family of the bride upon marriage in return for the loss of her labor

martial law: military control of a country during an emergency

military tribunal: a military court

militia: a group of people who train in military drills and keep weapons but who spend most of their time in civilian (nonmilitary) occupations, to be mobilized (called to military service) during emergencies

Trekkers: Dutch-speaking white settlers who left Cape Colony in the early 1800s to establish farms in areas of southern Africa outside of British control

ultimatum: a demand made under force of threat, where refusing the demand will result in the threatened action

Who's Who?

Bhambatha kaMancinza (ca. 1865–1906): This chief of the Zondi chiefdom in the Mpanza Valley ruled from the early 1890s to 1906, when he was removed as chief and replaced with his uncle, Magwababa. Bhambatha led the 1906 rebellion against the poll tax instituted in Natal-Zululand, claiming royal support and the royal battle cry of "uSuthu!" He died along with more than five hundred of his followers in the final confrontation between his army and government forces in the Mome Gorge in 1906. He was posthumously reinstated as chief in 2006.

Cetshwayo kaMpande (ca. 1832–1884): This Zulu king ruled from 1873 until 1884. Cetshwayo fought a battle for succession against his half brother Mbuyazi in 1856, and when his uSuthu party won, he became the unofficial Zulu leader. He reigned as king during the Anglo-Zulu War of 1879, and although he did not fight himself, he was commander in chief of the Zulu armies. Cetshwayo was captured by the British and exiled, only to be reinstated in 1883. He died in 1884 under somewhat mysterious circumstances (some claim a heart attack, others poisoning by his enemies).

Dinuzulu kaCetshwayo (1868–1913): Serving as Zulu king from 1884 until 1913, Dinuzulu was not recognized as king by Britain through much of his reign. He continued the fight between the uSuthu party and the Mandhlakazi that was sparked by the division of Zululand after the Anglo-Zulu War of 1879. He gave up a large portion of Zululand to the New Republic in return for assistance against the Mandhlakazi. He was exiled on St. Helena from 1890 until 1897 and returned to Zululand as chief and government induna and adviser. In 1907, the colonial authories again convicted him of treason for assisting rebels during the 1906 rebellion. Dinuzulu died in 1913 on the farm given to him by the government of the Union of South Africa.

John Dunn (1833–1895): This trader, son of British settlers in Natal, was one of the thirteen chiefs the British appointed to rule Zululand after the Anglo-Zulu War. Dunn lived most of his life among the Zulu people and often preferred their customs to those of Europeans. He sided with Mbuyazi in 1856. He and Mbuyazi were defeated by Cetshwayo, but Dunn soon became a trusted adviser to Cetshwayo, helping to arm his people. However, when the Anglo-Zulu War broke out, Dunn sided with the British and was rewarded with an independent chieftainship. He then sided with Zibhebhu in disputes with the uSuthu and died in retirement on his farm in 1895.

Mnyamana kaNgqengelele (ca. 1813–1892): One of Zulu king Cetshwayo's most important advisers, Mnyamana grew up during Shaka's reign and became Buthelezi chief during the reign of Mpande. He sided with Cetshwayo in 1856, and Cetshwayo appointed him head induna shortly after his coronation. Mnyamana consistently opposed white interference in Zululand, and although he surrendered to the British after the Battle of Ulundi, he was the only chief to refuse an appointed chieftainship after the Anglo-Zulu War. He was one of the most influential uSuthu leaders and strongly opposed dealing with Boers. In 1888, he refused to side against the powerful British, even allowing one of his impis to accompany forces sent against Dinuzulu's men. He died in 1892.

Ndabuko kaMpande (1847–ca. 1899): This Zulu prince and uSuthu leader was one of Cetshwayo's brothers. Ndabuko led protests against the appointed chiefs' mistreatment of the royal family and in favor of Cetshwayo's reinstatement while the king was in exile. He himself was exiled on St. Helena from 1890 until 1897 along with his brother Shingana and Dinuzulu.

Melmoth Osborn (1834–1899): Resident commissioner of Zululand, Osborn had served in the Natal government since he was a young man. He became a magistrate in Natal in 1867 and served until 1876 as colonial secretary with Theophilus Shepstone in the Transvaal in 1877. He became resident commissioner of Zululand after the Anglo-Zulu War and maintained a policy of supporting Zibhebhu and other enemies of the uSuthu as a counterbalance to a revival of the Zulu monarchy. He died in 1899.

Shaka kaSenzangakhona (ca. 1787–1828): Zulu king from 1816 until 1828, Shaka is seen as the father of the Zulu nation, although he never had any recognized children. An autocrat and military genius, Shaka completely changed Zulu society, and his military campaigns displaced groups throughout southeastern Africa. His innovations in weapons and tactics were used by the Zulu military throughout the nineteenth century. He also made use of the weapons of British traders whom he allowed to settle on his territory at Port Natal (what is modern-day Durban, South Africa). After losing the support of some of his people due to his excessively harsh rule, he was assassinated by his half brothers Dingane and Mhlangana in 1828.

Theophilus Shepstone (1817–1893): Originally from England, but raised in Cape Colony, Shepstone was secretary for native affairs in Natal from 1853 until 1875. In this position, he was one of the main developers of British policies toward local Africans in Natal. These policies included the hut tax and the system of government of local people by their own chiefs under white administrators. He saw the Zulu monarchy as a problem for Natal and attempted to reduce Cetshwayo's authority by gaining promises from him in return for British recognition of his kingship. Shepstone was one of the advisers who supported the creation of the thirteen chiefdoms following the Anglo-Zulu War. In 1877, he negotiated the annexation of the South African Republic to Britain and became its administrator. He died in 1893.

Sihayo kaXhongo (d. 1883): Chief of the Qungebe chiefdom in Zululand near Rorke's Drift, Sihayo supported Cetshwayo in the 1856 war and became one of Cetshwayo's favorites. Sihayo's sons were the cause of one of the incidents that led up to the Anglo-Zulu War. He himself commanded an impi at the Battle of Isandhlwana, and he and his son Mehlokazulu were captured during the war and taken prisoners. He died, along with many other notable Zulu leaders, in Zibhebhu's attack on Ulundi in 1883.

Zibhebhu kaMaphitha (1841–1904): Chief of the Mandlakazi and skilled Zulu general, Zibhebhu supported Cetshwayo in 1856 and attended his coronation. He participated in the Anglo-Zulu War, but he was offered an independent chieftainship because he surrendered after the Battle of Ulundi. He quickly became hated by the uSuthu for taking over the property and household members of the royal family and others associated with the uSuthu cause. Zibhebhu was the leader most opposed to the uSuthu movement after the Anglo-Zulu War and was the only appointed chief allowed to maintain an independent chiefdom after Cetshwayo's reinstallation in 1883. Zibhebhu was defeated by the Boers who came to assist the uSuthu at the battle of Tshaneni. When he was allowed to return to his lands after the British gained control, the hostility between the uSuthu and the Mandlakazi reignited. Zibhebhu was later arrested for murder. He died in 1904 at the point when old tensions between him and Dinuzulu were about to erupt again.

Source Notes

p. 9   Quoted in J. Ruscombe Poole, "Cetywayo's Story of the Zulu Nation and the War," *Macmillan's Magazine*, February 1880, 273–295 (repr., C. de B. Webb and J. B. Wright, eds., *A Zulu King Speaks: Statements Made by Cetshwayo kaMpande on the History and Customs of His People*. Pietermaritzburg: University of Natal Press, 1978), 10.

p. 11   Ibid., 13.

p. 12   British Parliamentary Papers, C.—2950, London, 1881, 129–139 (repr., C. de B. Webb and J. B. Wright, eds., *A Zulu King Speaks: Statements Made by Cetshwayo ka-Mpande on the History and Customs of His People*. Pietermaritzburg: University of Natal Press, 1978), 46.

p. 16   Charles Rowden Maclean, "Loss of the Brig *Mary* at Natal with Early Recollections of That Settlement and Among the Caffres," *Nautical Magazine*, 1853–1855 (repr., Maclean, *The Natal Papers of 'John Ross': Loss of the Brig Mary at Natal with Early Recollections of That Settlement and Among the Caffres*, ed. Stephen Gray. Pietermaritzburg: University of Natal Press, 1992), 84.

p. 17   Ibid., 18.

p. 18   Quoted in Frances Ellen Colenso, *The Ruin of Zululand: An Account of British Doings in Zululand Since the Invasion of 1879*, vol. 1 (London: William Ridgway, 1884), 267.

p. 19   Quoted in Colenso, *History of the Zulu War and Its Origin*, 239–240.

p. 20   Quoted in Frances Ellen Colenso, *The Ruin of Zululand: An Account of British Doings in Zululand Since the Invasion of 1879*, vol. 2 (London: William Ridgway, 1885), 15.

p. 21   Quoted in Poole, "Cetwayo's Story," repr., Webb and Wright, *A Zulu King Speaks*, 25.

p. 23   Ibid., 28–29.

p. 24   Ibid., 29.

p. 26   Ibid., 30.

p. 28   Quoted in Colenso, *The Ruin of Zululand*, 1: 265, 255.

p. 28   Ibid., 30–31.

p. 29   Ibid., 31.

p. 34   Quoted in Frances Ellen Colenso, *History of the Zulu War and Its Origin*, London: Chapman and Hall, 1880 (repr., Westport, CT: Negro Universities Press, 1970), 455.

p. 35   Ibid., 451.

p. 37   Ibid., 459.

p. 38   Quoted in Cornelius Vijn, *Cetshwayo's Dutchman: Being the Private Journal of a White Trader in Zululand During the British Invasion*, ed. and trans. J. W. Colenso (London: Longmans, Green, 1880; repr., New York: Negro Universities Press, 1969, 151).

p. 38	Ibid., 56.
p. 40	Ibid.
p. 40	Quoted in British Parliamentary Papers, 129–139 (repr., Webb and Wright, *A Zulu King Speaks*), 59.
p. 40	Ibid., 467.
p. 45	James Stuart, *A History of the Zulu Rebellion 1906 and of Dinuzulu's Arrest, Trial and Expatriation* (London: Macmillan, 1913; New York: Negro Universities Press, 1969), 14.
p. 45	Quoted in James Stuart, *The James Stuart Archive of Recorded Oral Evidence Relating to the History of the Zulu and Neighbouring Peoples*, vol. 4, ed. and trans. C. de B. Webb and J. B. Wright (Pietermaritzburg: University of Natal Press, 1976), 300.
p. 48	Quoted in Colenso, *The Ruin of Zululand*, 2:325.
p. 48	Ibid., 1: 151.
p. 49	Ibid., 1:52.
p. 50	Quoted in Poole, "Cetywayo's Story," repr., Webb and Wright, *A Zulu King Speaks*, 62.
p. 50	Ibid., 1:102.
p. 52	Ibid., 2:16.
p. 56	Ibid., 1:280.
p. 58	Quoted in Colenso, *The Ruin of Zululand*, 1:267.
p. 59	Ibid., 2:74.
p. 59	Ibid., 2:75.

p. 59   Quoted in Barry St.-John Nevill, ed., *Life at the Court of Queen Victoria 1861–1901* (Exeter, England: Webb & Bower, 1984), 111.

p. 60   Quoted in Colenso, *The Ruin of Zululand*, 2:84.

p. 60   Ibid., 2:64.

p. 60   Ibid., 2:76.

p. 60   Ibid., 2:84.

p. 61   Quoted in Colenso, *The Ruin of Zululand*, 2:433.

p. 61   Quoted in Nevill, *Life at the Court of Queen Victoria 1861–1901*, 111.

p. 62   Quoted in Colenso, *The Ruin of Zululand*, 2:9.

p. 62   Quoted in Nevill, *Life at the Court of Queen Victoria 1861–1901*, 2:228.

p. 63   Ibid., 2:217.

p. 64   Ibid., 2:305.

p. 65   Ibid., 2:275.

p. 65   Ibid., 2:292.

p. 66   Ibid., 2:347.

p. 66   Ibid., 2:340.

p. 67   Ibid., 2:408.

p. 68   Ibid.., 2:394.

p. 68   Ibid., 2:397.

p. 68   Ibid., 2:218.

p. 68   Ibid., 2:403.

p. 70   Ibid., 2:496.

p. 72   Ibid., 2:499.

p. 72   Ibid., 2:482.

p. 72   Quoted in James Stuart, *The James Stuart Archive of Recorded Oral Evidence Relating to the History of the Zulu and Neighbouring Peoples*, vol.3, ed. and trans. C. de B. Webb and J. B. Wright (Pietermaritzburg: University of Natal Press, 1982), 204.

p. 74   Quoted in R.C.A. Samuelson, *Long, Long Ago* (Durban: Knox, 1929), 122.

p. 89   Quoted in John Laband, *The Rise and Fall of the Zulu Nation* (London: Arms and Armour, 1997), 388.

p. 96   Stuart, *A History of the Zulu Rebellion 1906*, 92.

p. 96   Quoted in Stuart, *A History of the Zulu Rebellion 1906*, 16.

p. 98   Ibid.

p. 104   Ibid., 160.

p. 104   Ibid., 101.

p. 105   Ibid., 122.

p. 107   Quoted in Stuart, *A History of the Zulu Rebellion 1906*, 532.

p. 108   Ibid., 121.

p. 108   Ibid., 123.

p. 109	Quoted in Stuart, *The James Stuart Archive*, 1:307.
p. 110	Quoted in Samuelson, *Long, Long Ago*, viii.
p. 113	Ibid., 153.
p. 113	Ibid., 172–173.
p. 114	Quoted in Stuart, *A History of the Zulu Rebellion 1906*, 152.
p. 120	Ibid., 124.
p. 121	Quoted in Samuelson, *Long, Long Ago*, 202.

Bibliography

Binns, C.T. *Dinuzulu: The Death of the House of Shaka*. London: Longmans, 1968.

Bird, John, comp. *The Annals of Natal: 1495–1845*. Vol. 1. Cape Town: T. Maskew-Miller. Facsimile reprint, Cape Town: C. Struik, 1965.

———. *The Annals of Natal: 1495–1845*. Vol.2. Cape Town: T. Maskew-Miller. Facsimile reprint, Cape Town: C. Struik, 1965.

Cahoon, Benjamin M. "South African Traditional States." *Worldstatesmen.org*, 2000. <http://www.worldstatesmen.org/South_Africa_Bantu.html> (accessed February 25, 2008).

Churchill, Winston. *The Boer War: London to Ladysmith via Pretoria, Ian Hamilton's March*. London: Longman, Green, 1900. Reprint, New York: W. W. Norton, 1989.

CIA. "South Africa." *The World Factbook*. Updated March 15, 2007. <https://www.cia.gov/cia/publications/factbook/index.html> (accessed March 29, 2007).

Colenso, Frances. *Colenso Letters from Natal*. Edited by Wyn Rees. Pietermaritzburg: Shuter and Shooter, 1958.

———. *History of the Zulu War and Its Origin*. London: Chapman and Hall, 1880. Reprint, Westport, CT: Negro Universities Press, 1970.

———. *The Ruin of Zululand: An Account of British Doings in Zululand Since the Invasion of 1879*. Vol. 1. London: William Ridgway, 1884.

—————. *The Ruin of Zululand: An Account of British Doings in Zululand Since the Invasion of 1879.* Vol. 2. London: William Ridgway, 1885.

Cope, Trevor, ed. *Izibongo: Zulu Praise-Poems.* Compiled by James Stuart. Translated by Daniel Malcolm. Oxford: Clarendon, 1968.

Doyle, Arthur Conan. *The Great Boer War.* New York: McClure, Phillips, 1901.

Federal Research Division, Library of Congress. *South Africa: A Country Study.* Edited by Rita M. Byrnes. Washington, DC: U.S. Government Printing Office, 1997.

Hinsley, F. H., ed. *The New Cambridge Modern History: Volume XI Material Progress and World-Wide Problems, 1870–1898.* Cambridge: Cambridge University Press, 1967.

Isaacs, Nathaniel. *Travels and Adventures in Eastern Africa: Descriptive of the Zoolus, Their Manners, Customs with a Sketch of Natal.* Edited by Louis Herman and Percival R. Kirby. Cape Town: C. Struik, 1970. Originally published 1836 by Edward Churton, 26 Holles Street, London.

isiZulu.net Zulu-English/English-Zulu Online Dictionary, 2004–2008. <http://isizulu.net> (accessed March 17, 2007).

Knight, Ian. *The Anatomy of the Zulu Army from Shaka to Cetshwayo 1818–1879.* London: Greenhill, 1995.

—————. *Brave Men's Blood: The Epic of the Zulu War 1879.* Barnsley, South Yorkshire, England: Pen & Sword, 2005.

KwaZulu-Natal Provincial Government. *Bhambatha Centenary Commission,* 2006. <http://www.kwazulunatal.gov.za/bhambatha/background.htm> (accessed March 29, 2007).

—————. *State of the Province Address, 8 February 2006.* <http://www.kwazulunatal.gov.za/bhambatha/State_Province_Address/State_Province_Address.pdf> (accessed March 29, 2007).

Laband, John. *The Rise and Fall of the Zulu Nation.* London: Arms and Armour, 1997.

Maclean, Charles Rowden. "Loss of the Brig *Mary* at Natal with Early Recollections of That Settlement and Among the Caffres." *Nautical Magazine*, 1853–1855. Reprinted in *The Natal Papers of 'John Ross': Loss of the Brig Mary at Natal with Early Recollections of That Settlement and Among the Caffres*. Edited by Stephen Gray. Pietermaritzburg: University of Natal Press, 1992.

Mandela, Nelson. *Long Walk to Freedom*. Boston: Little, Brown, 1994.

Morgan, Kenneth O., ed. *The Oxford Illustrated History of Britain*. Oxford: Oxford University Press, 1984.

Morris, Donald R. *The Washing of the Spears: A History of the Rise of the Zulu Nation under Shaka and Its Fall in the Zulu War of 1879*. New York: Simon & Schuster, 1965.

Nevill, Barry St.-John, ed. *Life at the Court of Queen Victoria 1861–1901*. Exeter, England: Webb & Bower, 1984.

Pakenham, Thomas. *The Boer War*. New York: Random House, 1979.

Ross, Robert. *A Concise History of South Africa*. Cambridge: Cambridge University Press, 1999.

Samuelson, R.C.A. *Long, Long Ago*. Durban: Knox, 1929.

Soszynski, Henry. "Zulu (Nguni Tribe)." *Non-European Royalty, N.D.* <http://www.uq.net.au/~zzhsoszy/states/southafrica/zulu.html> (accessed February 25, 2008).

South African History Online. "King Goodwill Zwelithini 1948–, N.D." <http://www.sahistory.org.za/pages/people/bios/zwelithini-g.htm> (accessed March 29, 2007).

Stuart, James. *A History of the Zulu Rebellion 1906 and of Dinuzulu's Arrest, Trial and Expatriation*. London: Macmillan, 1913. Reprint, New York: Negro Universities Press, 1969.

———. *The James Stuart Archive of Recorded Oral Evidence Relating to the History of the Zulu and Neighbouring Peoples.* Vol.1. Edited and translated by C. de B. Webb and J. B. Wright. Pietermaritzburg: University of Natal Press, 1976.

———. *The James Stuart Archive of Recorded Oral Evidence Relating to the History of the Zulu and Neighbouring Peoples.* Vol. 2. Edited and translated by C. de B. Webb and J. B. Wright. Pietermaritzburg: University of Natal Press, 1976.

———. *The James Stuart Archive of Recorded Oral Evidence Relating to the History of the Zulu and Neighbouring Peoples.* Vol. 3. Edited and translated by C. de B. Webb and J. B. Wright. Pietermaritzburg: University of Natal Press, 1982.

———. *The James Stuart Archive of Recorded Oral Evidence Relating to the History of the Zulu and Neighbouring Peoples.* Vol. 4. Edited and translated by C. de B. Webb and J. B. Wright. Pietermaritzburg: University of Natal Press, 1986.

Thompson, Leonard. *A History of South Africa*, 3rd ed. New Haven: Yale University Press, 2000.

uMlalazi Tourism Association. "The Colonial Heritage: John Dunn—The White Chief of Zululand," N.D. <http://www.visitzululand.co.za/dunn.html#dunn> (accessed February 25, 2008).

Vijn, Cornelius. *Cetshwayo's Dutchman: Being the Private Journal of a White Trader in Zululand During the British Invasion.* Edited and translated by J. W. Colenso. London: Longmans, Green: 1880. Reprint, New York: Negro Universities Press, 1969.

Webb, C. de B., and J. B. Wright, eds. *A Zulu King Speaks: Statements Made by Cetshwayo kaMpande on the History and Customs of His People.* Pietermaritzburg: University of Natal Press, 1978.

Wilson, A. N. *The Victorians.* New York: W. W. Norton, 2003.

For Further Reading, Websites, and Movies

BOOKS

Finlayson, Reggie. *Nelson Mandela*. Minneapolis: Twenty-First Century Books, 1999.

Gleimius, Nita, Evelina Sibanyoni, and Emma Mthimunye. *The Zulu of Africa*. Minneapolis: Lerner, 2003.

Hamilton, Janice. *South Africa in Pictures*. Minneapolis: Twenty-First Century Books, 2004.

Knight, Ian. *The Anatomy of the Zulu Army from Shaka to Cetshwayo 1818–1879*. London: Greenhill, 1995.

————. *Brave Men's Blood: The Epic of the Zulu War 1879*. Barnsley, South Yorkshire, England: Pen & Sword, 2005.

Mandela, Nelson. *Long Walk to Freedom*. Boston: Little, Brown, 1994.

Morris, Donald R. *The Washing of the Spears: A History of the Rise of the Zulu Nation under Shaka and Its Fall in the Zulu War of 1879*. Cambridge: Da Capo, 1998.

Reader's Digest. *Illustrated History of South Africa: The Real Story*. Cape Town: Reader's Digest Association Limited, 1994.

Thompson, Leonard. *A History of South Africa*, 3rd ed. New Haven: Yale University Press, 2000.

WEBSITES

isiZulu.net Zulu-English/English-Zulu Online Dictionary
<http://isizulu.net>.
This is a worthwhile site for those interested in isiZulu, the Zulu
language, containing a searchable dictionary, a grammar guide,
audio samples of pronunciation, and more.

KwaZulu-Natal Provincial Government
<http://www.kwazulunatal.gov.za>.
The official site of the government of the province of KwaZulu-Natal
is a source of information about the issues facing the area that
was once Zululand.

Royal Engineers Museum: "Engineers and the Zulu War of 1879"
<http://www.remuseum.org.uk/campaign/rem_campaign_zulu
war79.htm>.
This site provides many technical details about the Anglo-Zulu War,
with summaries of battles, pictures, and eyewitness quotes.

South African History Online
<http://www.sahistory.org.za>.
This project is devoted to developing a nonpartisan history of the
people of South Africa, containing a wealth of information on
the history of South Africa.

vgsbooks.com
<http://www.vgsbooks.com.
Visit vgsbooks.com, the homepage of the visual Geography Series®,
which is updated regularly. You can get linked to all sorts of use-
ful on-line information, including geographical, historical, demo-
graphic, cultural, and economic websites. The vgsbooks.com site is
a great resource for late-breaking news and statistics about a variety
of nations, including South Africa.

Zulu Kingdom

<http://www.kzn.org.za/kzn>.

Primarily a site promoting tourism, Zulu Kingdom also provides succinct summaries of matters in Zulu history, including summaries of the major battles of the Anglo-Zulu War.

MOVIES

Shaka Zulu. DVD. Directed by William C. Faure. With Henry Cele, Edward Fox, Kenneth Griffith, Gordon Jackson, and Dudu Mkhize. A&E Home Video 1983. A ten-part television miniseries about the rise and fall of Shaka that basically attempts to portray the history, although liberties are taken for dramatic effect. Filmed in South Africa before the end of apartheid, the series attempts to balance black and white views of the founder of the Zulu nation.

Zulu. DVD. Directed by Cy Endfield. With Stanley Eakes, Jack Hawkins, and Michael Caine. Narrated by Richard Burton. MGM, 1964. A classic film about the defense of Rorke's Drift, where a small contingent of British soldiers held out against a Zulu army who had disobeyed Cetshwayo's orders and crossed over into Natal. Although fictionalized, many of the events depicted in the film are true to history.

Zulu Dawn. DVD. Directed by Douglas Hickox. With Burt Lancaster, Peter O'Toole, Simon Ward, and Simon Sabela. Tango Entertainment, 1979. A film about the Battle of Isandhlwana and the events leading up to it, including the contrast between the attitudes of the officials in Natal and those of the queen. Like most historical films, some liberties are taken, but *Zulu Dawn* provides a good feel for the situations surrounding the British defeat at Isandhlwana. 1979.

Zulu Wars. DVD. Directed by Richard Charles Wawman. Narrated by John Hurt. Good Times Video, 2003. A collection of three documentaries with reenactments of battles in Zulu history, featuring interviews with descendants of key figures and commentary by scholars of Zulu military history. *Shaka—King of the Zulu* describes the rise of Shaka; *Blood River*, the encounters between Zulu and Boer forces, the Battle of Blood River in particular; and *Red Coat, Black Blood*, the Anglo-Zulu War.

Index

Sigananda (Zulu chief), 114, 115
Sihayo (Zulu chief), sons of, 19, 39
smallpox, 63
Sokhexe, Battle of, 24
Solomon (Nkayishana, son of Dinuzulu), 128
South Africa Act (1909), 122
South African Republic (Transvaal): Anglo-Boer War, 98–100; annexed by Great Britain, 99; founded, 12; independence, 52. *See also* Transvaal
South African War (1899-1902), 98–100
St. Helena, 93–94
Stuart, James, 95–96, 98
surrender terms, 36–38
Swazi, war with, 21

taxes: hut, 86, 88, 103; poll, 103–105, 106–111
tick fever, 100
Times of Natal (newspaper), 70
Transvaal, 18, 51–52, 122
Trewirgie, incident at, 108–111
Tshaneni, Battle of, 77–78

Ulundi, Battle of, 4–6, 31–34
Union of South Africa, 122–128
uSuthu: appeals to British for redress, 48–51; attacked by warriors of Zibhebhu, 70–72; Battle of Tshaneni, 77–78; beginning of, 47; and Boers, 74–75, 81–82; and death of Cetshwayo, 73; in former territory of Zibhebhu, 90; name derivation, 13; opposition to Zululand as British protectorate, 88–92; and return of Cetshwayo to throne, 65–66; support for, 55; and Zulu Native Reserve, 68, 75–76

Victoria (queen of England), 54, 55, 59, 61
Vijn, Cornelius, 4, 38, 40

Wheelwright, William, 46
Wolsely, Sir Garnet: appointed, 34–35; on Cetshwayo's return to throne, 61; on Hamu, 47; plan for Zulus, 43–46; terms of surrender offered by, 36–38
Wood, Henry Evelyn, 29, 48–49

Zibhebhu: appointed chief by British, 45; army of, 70; banned from former lands, 95; cattle raids by, 69; and demands of Boers, 75; and Dinuzulu, 38, 45, 70–72, 77–78, 91–92; return of, 89, 98; and return of Cetshwayo to throne, 62–63, 68; supported by Osborn, 50, 51; Zulu opinion of, 67–68
Zululand: British protection of, 18, 20, 76, 87–88; census, 103, 104; division of, 60, 61–63; early years of kingdom, 7–10; invasion of, 24; living conditions in, 16, 81, 95, 98, 101, 105, 106; and Natal, 11, 85–86, 96, 98, 100; poll tax, 103–105, 106–111; return of Cetshwayo to, 55, 64–66; return of Dinuzulu to, 97; and treaty between New Republic and Great Britain, 83–85; and Wolseley's terms of surrender, 37–38
Zulu Native Reserve (the Reserve), 62–63, 68–69, 75–76
Zulus: culture, 100–102 (*See also* cattle); famine, 95–96, 105; Inkatha established, 125; on land granted to Boers, 81; lifestyle in early 19th century of, 16; marriage customs, 11, 16, 21, 50, 96; and military alliances, 75; and modern KwaZulu-Natal, 128–129; in Natal, 85
Zulu warrriors: beliefs of, 27; and Cetshwayo return to throne, 70–72; characteristics of, 6; desire for war, 20–21, 31; training of, 10, 11; weapons, 28, 45, 108, 109, 111; in Wolseley plan, 44. *See also specific battles*

Photo Acknowledgments

The images in this book are used with the permission of: © Mary Evans Picture Library/The Image Works, 5, 14, 36, 79/© The British Library/HIP/The Image Works, 8/Hulton Archive/Getty Images, 15, 67, 82, 93, 110, 123/© The Print Collector/Alamy, 27, 49, 59, 81/HIP/Art Resource, N.Y., 39/The Battle of Isandlwana: The Last Stand of the 24th Regiment of Foot (South Welsh Borderers) during the Zulu War, 22nd January 1879, c.1885 (oil on canvas), Fripp, Charles Edwin (1854-1906), The Art Archive/National Army Museum/London, 29/The Defence of Rorke's Drift, 1880 (oil on canvas), Neuville, Alphonse Marie de (1835-85)/Art Gallery of New South Wales, Sydney, Australia, The Bridgeman Art Library, 30/ © Corbis, 42, 86, 107/AKG-Images, Inc., 44/© Hulton-Deutsch Collection/Corbis, 46, 54, 119/© Roger Viollet/The Image Works, 53/© The Illustrated London News/Mary Evans Picture Library, 64, 67/© World History Archive/Alamy, 71,/© Mary Evans Picture Library, 89/© INTERPHOTO/Pressebildagentur/Alamy, 94/ © The Print Collector/Heritage Images/The Image Works, 102, 105/(gouache on paper), McConnell, James Edwin (1903-95)/Private Collection, © Look and Learn/ The Bridgeman Art Library, 116/© Anthony Bannister; Gallo Images/Corbis, 125/© Reuters/Corbis, 127.

Front Cover: © Bettmann/Corbis

About the Author

Matthew S. Weltig began his career studying East Asia. He later taught there for several years, then returned to the United States to study and teach language as a university lecturer. Weltig works in the field of language testing and learning. He also writes on topics in world history. He lives with his wife Yan in Monterey, California.